# My Pet Connection

## *Inspirational 'Tails' of Adoption*

Joe Kirchmyer

Copyright © 2017 Joe Kirchmyer
Printed in the United States of America

Kirchmyer, Joe

My Pet Connection: Inspirational 'Tails' of Adoption/ Kirchmyer- 1st Edition

ISBN: 978-0-9996208-1-6


1. My Pet Connection   2. Pet Adoption   3. Nonfiction
4. Pets  5. Kirchmyer

NFB Publishing
119 Dorchester Road
Buffalo, New York 14213

For more information visit
nfbpublishing.com

*My Pet Connection: Inspirational 'Tails' of Adoption*

Located in the small town of Marilla, New York, Pet Connection Programs Inc. is a nonprofit maternity shelter for dogs and cats. Founded in 1984, the shelter has saved thousands of animals that simply had no other place to go. Following are dozens of those stories. Some will make you laugh, some will make you cry … and all will warm your heart!

To learn more about the shelter and ways that you can help, please visit their website at www.petconnectionprogramsinc.com. And to contact Pet Connection Programs Inc., please email petadoption652@gmail.com or call (716) 652-0192.

This book is dedicated to all the animals that have made my life much more enjoyable, including Peanuts, Smokey, Allie, Rudy, Brownie, Bandit, Tyson, Cooper and Chance!

— Joe Kirchmyer

# BAILEY

We had been talking about getting a dog and were looking in the paper for puppies. I had to go to the pet store for something for my cat and there was a poster up about puppies to adopt the very next day. So, we took a trip that Saturday in February 2011.

We didn't think we would come home with a dog that day so we were pleasantly surprised when we did. My husband reminds me that he picked out our Bailey from the group. We chose Bailey as a name because her blonde hair reminded us of Bailey's Irish Creme. We were told she was a Shepard mix and she looked very much so. As she's grown, the black on her back has faded and she looks more like a lean and slender hound.

From the first day we took her home she wanted to be right next to us. The first night she slept in a crate and cried when she went to bed. She settled back in and then cried again very early. The next night we knew we both had to work Monday and we wanted to try and see if she would sleep through the night in the bed. She slept between our heads the entire night without making a peep. She's slept in the bed ever since and wouldn't understand how to sleep anywhere else. She's spoiled and we let it happen.

Bailey is the happiest, sweetest dog ever. She is our baby and absolutely loves almost everything. She will just start running when she gets into an open area and tires herself out. We have an Invisible Fence in our yard so she has plenty of room to run whenever she wants. She also loves swimming and hunting for rabbits, chipmunks and squirrels.

As active as she is even at six years old, she always needs to cuddle at the end of the day or when we have blankets. She will pile up the blankets and looks like the princess that she is.

Getting her from Pet Connection was one of our best decisions ever. They made it so easy to adopt. We are lucky to have such a loyal and happy dog. Seriously, who rescued who?

— Sarah Franklin

# BARKLEY

Shortly before Thanksgiving our family went out to dinner at a restaurant next door to a PetSmart where Pet Connection was holding an adoption event. We stopped in after dinner and there were a whole bunch of frolicking puppies running around yipping and playing. Amid all the chaos lay a tiny black pup with a white splotch on it's chest, four legs splayed in all directions ... and it was hiccuping!

My son Matthew instantly fell in love! I had gone in to pick up something for our dog at home, Buddy, when Matthew came up to me cradling the sleeping pup in his arms. "Dad said to ask you. I don't want anything else for Christmas! Can we get it?" He then carried this puppy around the store for forty-five minutes!

My husband and daughter Katie immediately joined in and campaigned for the adoption. After a resounding chorus of "Please, please, please," the answer came ..."Get out the credit card!"

Katie and I were excited to have another girl in the family and picked out a cute collar and leash set while my husband and son filled out the adoption paperwork. We went to collect our new family member but they gave us the wrong puppy! Turns out the puppy my son carried for forty-five minutes was a boy! We picked out a new collar and leash, returned the pink set and headed to the van with our new puppy!

Missing from this whole adventure was our oldest son, Michael, who had gone into another store. He was in for quite the surprise when he hopped into the van and discovered our new puppy!

Barkley has now been a member of the Krygier family for over seven years!

— Laurie Krygier

# BELLA

In March 2011, I lost my twelve-year-old Lab to an illness. My family was sad and I had no plan on getting another dog for a while.

I was at a local mall on a Saturday to do some shopping and I walked into an area that was having an animal adoption fair. I was still sad from my loss. A woman handed my a leash and I could not help myself and cried.

When I got home I told my family that life wouldn't be the same without a dog to love, so I began my search for a new family member. I looked online and asked around about a shelter I could trust to adopt a dog from. While on Petfinder.com I came across Pet Connection and liked what I read and saw, so I called to see where they were located.

It was like fate brought me there. My aunt is buried nearby and she was a true dog lover. All I could think of was she helped me find Pet Connection. I called and made an appointment to fill out an application.

My dad and I went to Pet Connection on April 19, 2011, to see a few litters of puppies. We instantly found a new member to complete our family. She was the only one not sleeping in her group and came right over to us. We knew at that exact moment that this was our new dog.

What an amazing and loving dog she has grown to be, and such a great part of our family! Thanks to Pet Connection for what you do to help and adopt out animals. My dog's name is Bella.

— Renee Sundquist

# BELLA

I've been a cat person most of my life. I feel that there's nothing more soothing than the sound of a purr. I still feel that way but I had a bit of ill health come my way and felt lonely while recuperating. I needed more companionship than a cat can offer because a cat wants attention only when they want it, so I thought about getting a dog to go for walks with me and to get me back to feeling better after my illness.

When I was a kid my grandparents raised German Shepherds and I had very fond memories of them. I started looking for dogs that needed homes in the Western New York area and somehow came upon Pet Connection in Marilla.

There happened to be two German Shepherds there so I emailed them and set up an appointment to look at the pups. I had never been to Marilla before and my Garmin was acting up; suddenly it would stop working but somehow I made it to the appointment.

My husband was also working in the area that day so he was able to take a break and look at the pups (we can never plan anything together because of work conflicts). Well, we got to meet a bunch of cute little ones that day. Most were fighting for our attention but there was one little shy girl that stayed away from the group. Every time I looked over her way she was looking at me so I picked her up and she had the sweetest face I ever saw. My husband was holding one of the little Shepherds. There was a brother and sister and they were adorable and they wanted to go home with us but I looked over and the little girl was looking at me like she had met me before and knew she would be coming home with me.

On the way home, I got tears in my eyes thinking about the little Border Collie Lab mix so my husband and I talked about it and I called Julie and told her I wanted to pick up the little puppy formerly known as Gem. Julie told me to come and get her the very next day so I headed out to Marilla with my Garmin and picked her up.

She was so little that I put her in a cat carrier for the drive home. Pet Connection gave me a little starter pack with some puppy food, but once I got home I realized she didn't have any toys or leashes or a harness so we went to Petco. I put her in the cart and we had a great time shopping. People at the store loved her and a guy who worked there asked if he could smell her because she had "the new puppy smell."

I put her harness and leash on which she really didn't like at first and we walked around the border of our yard. She thought it was weird of me to hang out with her when she had to relieve herself, and she likes to run to the other side of the house now that she's older to have private bathroom time.

The first time I saw my puppy smile was when my husband and I were running along the border of our yard and she looked up at us. She seemed so happy and that cuteness is burned into my memory.

We go for walks and she also likes to take drives and catch Frisbees. She is very smart and she likes to be helpful, too. I had to fence in my garden because she wanted to help me with my vegetables.

Her name is Bella now and she's a great dog with the happiest wagging tail I've ever seen. Her birthday is March 18, 2012.

I feel that creatures need to be around their own kind so I started looking at Pet Connection again in 2013. See Teddy's story later in this book for the continuation!

— Terri Smith

# BROOKE

Let me tell you about Brooke. I adopted Brooke five years ago when I saw her on Pet Connection's website. It was New Year's Day and I called thinking I would get a message. It just so happened that someone was there and I talked to them. I thought, "Wow, this is a sign." The more we talked I knew I had to go and meet her, which I did the very next day. Of course I fell in love and brought her home.

Brooke has been a pure joy. She lives in Depew with my son and I and she is the sweetest dog. She is just so happy to lay on the sofa with you, lay in bed with my son or sit right next to you. She just loves to be loved and we love to love her back.

Every morning my son comes in from work at 2:30 a.m. and has to sit on the floor next to Brooke's bed and pet her before he does anything else. She loves to go for walks and is so well behaved. She is a great companion and there is nothing I would change about her. She is a loving family member.

— Kathie Kimmel

# BUDDY

I adopted a puppy twelve years ago from the Buffalo Animal Shelter. Her name was Lucy, and she was found in a cardboard box in a back yard on the East Side of Buffalo. She was listed as a "Shepherd mix" breed but as she grew, there was no mistaking she was actually a Pit Bull.

Pit Bulls get a bad rap, but she was the most loyal and affectionate dog I've ever known. She was by my side through so many chapters — divorce, the trials and tribulations of raising young children, remarriage, a fourth child — and then she became ill. When she crossed the rainbow bridge, I was devastated and swore that I would never have another dog … until I stumbled upon a Facebook post from Pet Connections Programs Inc. in Marilla with pictures of three litters of puppies.

I couldn't stop visiting the site and looking at the pictures of these lovable puppies. I responded to the Facebook post and received a message to complete an extensive adoption application. I was at the gym when I received a call that we had 45 minutes to get to Marilla from West Seneca on a Sunday. I picked up my husband and children and we headed to

Marilla for a meet-and-greet.

When we arrived, there were twelve puppies snoozing, playing, eating and just being absolutely adorable! After playing with these puppies and seeing my husband and children interact with one dog in particular, there was no doubt in my mind that our family was ready to grow!

One little four-pound puppy sought us out and stayed by my youngest son's side the entire time. He followed him everywhere. We were sitting outside with some pups and he jumped on my husband's lap. He jumped into my arms and cuddled into my shoulder. He chose us!

While filling out the paperwork to take the puppy home, the volunteer asked what we were going to name the dog. Immediately my son replied, "Buddy!" The dog jumped into his arms as if he approved. The name suits him perfectly. He is so friendly and is truly everyone's "Buddy!"

Welcoming a pet into our family was a big decision, but life is better than ever with the companionship of our new best friend, our "Buddy."

— Lisa Chrapowicz

# BUG

We adopted Bug on January 1, 2015. She had puppies and was a little thin. The process to adopt her was easy and we knew she would fit in with our family and our other dog, Molly, right away. She was quiet and a little nervous.

She is a quiet dog and a couch potato. She was eight when we got her and ten now. We love her and are making her life now as comfortable as we can. She stays with us outside and likes to move around nonchalantly when we go for walks. Her favorite things to do are eating and sleeping.

I have no idea what her first eight years were like, but we think she's the cat's pajamas and she thinks she died and went to heaven.

— Lynn and Chuck Pautler

# BURTON

I will never forget the day my sister and I went to Pet Connection to see the Lab mix puppies. My sister was looking for a puppy, but not me. My own "puppies" were just staring to become independent and did not need their mother so much. With my daughter in high school and a son in college, I was starting to adjust to the empty nest ... until I went to Pet Connection.

Visiting with all the dogs was fun. I had forgotten what unconditional love felt like, and all these dogs just wanted love and attention. I kind of knew how they felt as my kids were never around and they didn't like me to hug and kiss them in front of their friends anymore. Maybe I would consider an older dog. There were so many older animals that needed good homes. They don't need as much attention and don't have the crazy energy like a puppy. An older dog would be good company for me. I made up my mind — an older dog it is!

Then we went into the puppy room and it was crazy. There were two litters — eight black Labs and four grey and white pups that looked like wolves. My sister and I sat down in the middle of the pups to play. They all were wild and really cute. One black Lab came over to me and climbed into my lap and kissed me. I would put him down and he would climb right back into my lap and demand my attention. I have had puppies and dogs before but I never had one that just refused to leave me alone. The rest of the puppies had an attention span of about 15 seconds — they were happy with anyone's attention and they had each other to play with — but this puppy just wanted me.

I remember thinking I'd better get out of here before it was too late. This puppy was needy. I got up and put him down and was leaving … and he started to whimper. I looked at him, our eyes locked and I knew we were in love and were meant to be.

That was eight years ago and Burton has truly never left my side. He likes kids and he is friendly to everyone but he wants to be with me all the time. We have two very loving cats and my son has his own dog now but Burton will not allow them anywhere near me and if they sneak up on my lap Burton will nudge them away. I am so happy that I adopted Burton and I can't imagine life without him.

We really have a "pet connection!"

— Anne McGillicuddy

# BUSS

In June 2009, our dog Dakota was hit by a car and our family was very sad. A few days later, we went to search for a new family pet and went to Pet Connection. We looked at and played with all kinds of dogs. We liked the Lab puppies but because our Creed was only a few months old, we knew we couldn't get a puppy. We saw some other dogs that seemed nice but decided we would keep looking to find the perfect one.

As we were about to leave, someone at Pet Connection said, "Oh, you should meet Lexi before you leave." She was out for a walk at the time so we waited a few minutes until Lexi, a full-grown Husky/Terrier mix, came back from her walk. She walked right up and licked Aurora across the face and we knew right away that she was a member of our family.

Lexi was rescued by Pet Connection from a shelter in Ohio where she was found wandering on a rural road. Nobody knows how old she is or anything about her before she was found by the Richland County, Ohio, dog warden.

We brought Lexi home a few days later to be with her family — mom, dad, Aurora (2-1/2) and Creed (three months). Since there were several other Lexi's already in the neighborhood, we decided to give her a new name. Aurora named her Buss.

Buss now has a dog sister, Tia, a yellow Lab (also a rescue) and a brother, Papi, a Chihuahua. They have an acre and a half to run, play and dig holes within their Invisible Fence area.

Although Buss is the boss of the group, she loves her brother and sister and human family and has even played with other animals that wander into the yard including deer, raccoons, opossum, beaver, a coyote and even a skunk. She even played tag with a skunk a few times which meant she had to have a special bath so she could come back in the house. She was seen running down the driveway side-by-side with her friend, the skunk.

Buss loves winter and when there is a lot of snow she loves to play king of the mountain on the snow pile on our back deck. She won't let her brother or sister sit on top of the pile with her.

Unlike her brother and sister, Buss has no interest in toys. She just likes running around and playing outside. With her long white and black fur, Buss is always with us. Even though we bought her a comfy bed after we brought her home, she spends her nights on the floor in the bedroom sleeping with her head under her dad's side of the bed. She is the happiest dog in the world and gives her family that same happiness.

— Scott Livingstone

# BUSTER

Almost two years ago, after not having a dog for the first time in my life, it was time to adopt. I saw that Pet Connection had a three-year-old part Terrier looking for a home. I always tried to get an older dog that needed a good home, and always Terriers since I love that breed.

Well, when we walked in, here is this little part Hound puppy looking at us like, "Are you here to play with me?" My husband fell in love right away and I was trying to talk him out of a puppy.

"What, are you nuts? A puppy!"

The girl said, "Why don't you just hold him?" I said, "No thank you."

"Oh, come on," she said. "No, I know what will happen if I do."

Well, I finally did and when he put his head on my shoulder and just sighed, it was all over for me. So that is how we adopted Buster. When we first brought him home I told my husband I thought he was sick because he was so quiet and just laying around. But he said, "No, it's just that you are used to having Terriers, and he's part Hound." And he has been that laid back ever since.

There hasn't been a day that I regret getting our Buster, so thanks Pet Connection for giving us a perfect dog!

— Birde Clarkson

# CHELSEA

Our Cairn Terrier Mandy passed away on December 2, 2012, after a wonderful life. My niece, Makena, was born eleven days later on December 13. I was at college and did not have the opportunity to say goodbye to Mandy. I graduated in the Spring of 2013 and knew I would be living at home and had a work schedule that would allow someone to be home with a dog at most times during the day and night. I really wanted my own dog. My parents said as long as it was a rescue I could adopt a dog. I quickly found Pet Connection and a litter whose mother was a Puggle/Boxer mix. We believe that she also has some Pit Bull in her, too.

After being approved for adoption the day came to head to Marilla to pick out the puppy. I was not able to get off of work so my dad, mom, sister, cousin and Makena went to pick out the puppy. They picked out two puppies and sent pictures of which I said either was fine. They decided that they would let the puppy pick us. They put Makena in the pen and this one adorable puppy with a white streak down its nose and a white chest cuddled right up to her. Without a doubt she was the one. To this day Makena and Chelsea are the best of friends.

Chelsea, named after my favorite soccer team, loves to watch television. Some of her favorites are watching hockey and soccer, but she enjoys almost any show, especially anything with other animals. My family discovered very quickly just how smart Chelsea is as it only took a few accidents in the house after we got her home and she was potty trained. She also chews her own nails down so no trips to the vet to have them clipped.

In the winter she loves to go out to run and play in the snow. In the summer she likes playing in the little pool and drinking from the hose. However, she is not very fond of going out when it's raining. She's a huge socialite, particularly when we go on walks. It is almost a necessity to stop and say hi to anyone we meet along the way. When something scares her (howling winds, thunder, rain) she either hides in her crate or behind my father's chair. As you can see by the picture, she has also become good friends with our sixteen-year-old cat.

Chelsea has been a joyful addition to our family and brings us lots of love every single day. She also smiles (she actually scrunches her nose so it looks like she is smiling). We are so thankful for the work Pet Connection does to care for rescue animals!

— Chris Loucks

# CINNAMON

I grew up with cats in the house but I never actually got to choose the cat. Cats always found us, showing up as fully grown strays in need of a family. A few years had passed without a cat in the house and I started to feel the need to adopt a kitten. I had visions of a sweet ball of fur napping on my lap or frolicking with the little toys I bought it.

While I had decided that I wanted an orange kitten with white paws, I wasn't actively searching. One day in December 2008, I came across a picture of an inquisitive-looking orange Tabby kitten on the Pet Connection website and I knew he was the one. As soon as we walked into the shelter, there he was, hanging on the front of his cage.

I filled out the adoption form while he chewed the zipper pull off of my coat, and named him Cinnamon. We brought him home, he hopped out of his carrier, and the house and all of its contents were immediately under his control. Humans and dogs were there to serve and entertain him. Every nook and cranny needed to be explored and every movable object needed to be pushed over. But he was also adorable and sweet when he wanted to be.

We filled the house with toys to entertain him and played with him for hours before bedtime in hopes of getting a good night's sleep. In return, he played with the loudest "trash" he could find all night long while singing a high-pitched song.

Those first few weeks (months if we're being honest) were definitely a learning experience. The humans and dog learned how to coexist and be bossed around by a four-pound ball of fur. Cinnamon learned his boundaries and settled into a quiet life as my mother's constant companion. Now nine years later, Cinnamon is still the boss of the house but I can't imagine life without him.

— Katherine Winkler

# CLEO

I first met Cleo when Pet Connection brought her to the vet clinic I work at in April of 2009. We estimated her to be about six years old with multiple health problems including dental disease, a bad elbow and kidney disease.

She was brought here from a shelter in Ohio and she had a large litter of puppies in March 2009. All of Cleo's puppies got forever homes but she was still at the shelter due to her health problems. I knew she would fit in perfectly with our family. I was prepared for her medical needs but I wasn't prepared for how this amazing dog would change my life.

Cleo loved to cuddle and go on walks with the dog next door. She even cuddled with the cat and was great company for my elderly uncle. Cleo was my emotional support during a rough time in my life. She was also a great judge of character; if she didn't like someone, which was rare, it was for a good reason.

Her kidney disease ultimately took her from us. Cleo was a wonderful dog and is still missed every day.

— Kelly Jakubczak

# CONNOR

We adopted Connor, whose name was Socks at the time, two years ago as a Father's Day present. I was diagnosed with PTSD-related anxiety and stress from multiple deployments and had read that a puppy was a good way to help alleviate stress and cope with anxiety. Socks came running out of the group of puppies right into my arms and I knew this energetic little guy was the one.

Connor has become as much a part of our family as any other member. He keeps me smiling when I'm feeling stressed and he cuddles up with the kids when they're feeling sick. He also loves swimming in the pool!

He's a great dog and a big goof, and I wouldn't change it for anything in the world. I'm so glad we decided to adopt from Pet Connection!

— Tad Wesser

# COSMO & DELTA

Our family has adopted two of our dogs from the Pet Connection: Cosmo, who we adopted as a puppy, and Delta, one of the mama dogs. They are such an important part of our little family.

Over ten years ago our family consisted of my husband Justin and our dog Klinger, our sweet and stubborn Basset Hound mix. My mom had found Klinger available in an ad in the newspaper. We wound up taking her. Life was pretty routine. I, however, was hoping to add another dog. It took me a good year to convince Justin to get on board.

I still remember that night at the rescue. There was a pile of pups, but one stuck out to me. She was black and white. She didn't have a tail, more of a nub. She was a sweetie and the only one that was awake. She responded to us and came running back when I called her. Cosmo is a herding dog mix.

Cosmo was an energetic puppy and she and Klinger hit it off very well. She cried at night and I grabbed her and threw her under the blankets with us. Ten years later guess where she still sleeps? Cosmo also loves people. She just wants to be near us at all times. When friends or family come over she has to hop on their laps.

I'm probably her favorite human. I suffer from Type 1 Diabetes. Sometimes at night my blood sugar will drop and Justin will have to help me ingest some juice or candy. This dog will not leave my side! I always feel her right by my side.

In the next five years we added one more dog, Penny, who Justin found outside one winter day. Penny is our Beagle mix. We had no luck tracking down any owners so we decided to add her to the family. We also had a human addition, our only child, Caroline. I love that she has all of these dogs.

Life continued on and Klinger was almost twelve. Last fall she was sick with pancreatitis, and a couple of weeks later I really thought she was getting better. Sadly, in early December, she passed away very suddenly. We lost her as my hand was on my phone to call our vet. We were heartbroken.

The house was so much quieter despite the two dogs. I would get up and hug the empty spot on the couch were she would sleep.

I am a frequent visitor to the Pet Connection website. There was a mama dog that had caught my eye earlier this year. It was Delta and I still remember her writeup: Hound mix, a sweetheart, on the goofy side, short tail, loves the other dogs, smiles when you talk to her. Some people may think it was too soon, but Klinger was always so good with the new dogs and I truly believe she was OK with us filling up her empty spot with another who needed a home.

I found myself in that familiar spot of bugging Justin for another dog. This time it only took about five weeks.

I still remember our meet and greet. Delta ran right up to us smiling. I felt connected to her immediately. She has been with us almost a year now.

Delta is, of course, a sweetheart. She's also a bit goofy. She sleeps with her chin on my leg. Like Cosmo, I feel that these dogs know I was the one pulling to go rescue them. We fell in love with Delta right off the bat.

So life goes on and Justin says no more dogs. For now ...

— Laurel Schmitz and Family

# CRUISER

Cruiser was adopted by our family on February 18, 2006, and we were told his mother was brought up from Hurricane Katrina! He is a black Lab/Chow mix and has the dark spots on his tongue to prove it.

He was a timid little guy and settled in quickly with our older Pet Connection adopted family member, Thunder. Thunder taught Cruiser so much of what he knows now and was the best decision we ever made. Cruiser has had a life of daily walks, learning countless tricks, opening Christmas and birthday presents, Milk-Bone biscuits, a plastic tub with his hundreds of toys, cuddling under a blanket we always put on him on cold nights, never being crated, enjoying the scents and sights of our mom's flower gardens, and free reign of couches and beds. He has a heart of gold and the sweetest spirit.

We just celebrated Cruiser's eleventh birthday and he unfortunately has had some health issues that we recently helped him surpass in his older age. As dogs get older, their bodies change and different problems can occur. Cruiser recently had to have minor surgery due to melanoma (which he is now free of) and knee surgery shortly after that. He has fully recovered from both and is loving life again and feels like himself.

We love him just as much as the day we got him. We celebrate his birthday every year with gifts to open, a ride in the car (maybe a McDonald's burger) and a cake … because he is our world as much as we are his. Cruiser is full of life just as much today as the day we adopted him despite all he's been through.

We could honestly write a novel about him and to sum it up in 500 words was almost next to impossible. We are so grateful for what Pet Connection does for these pets that need homes, and they have truly impacted our lives for the better. We wish he could be in our lives forever but it's a hard truth to have to accept that he can't, so we can only give him and all rescues the best lives they can possibly have for as long as we can.

We believe that adopting/rescuing one dog will not change the world, but for that one dog, his world will change forever!

— Donna Czechowski and her daughters Nicole, Ashley and Danielle (written by Danielle)

# DAISY

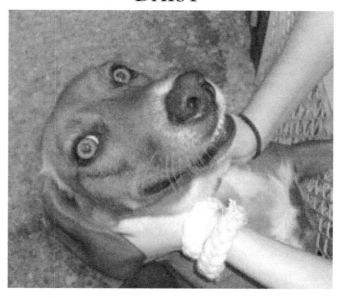

In the summer of 2009 I decided that it was time for another dog. Our previous dog lost her battle to cancer the previous summer and I missed having a walking buddy. When I shared this desire with my children they were thrilled. However, I did not want to start with a puppy again. This time I wanted an adult dog. I figured I could go to the SPCA and see what they had.

My son's friend, Katie, volunteered at Pet Connection. She told me that she walks the dogs and to my surprise, Pet Connection was about five minutes from my house. I had no idea it was even there.

Since my son selected our previous dog, my daughter Jessica got to select our new one. So Katie took us to Pet Connection. While I was en-amored with a black Lab, Jess fell in love with Daisy.

Daisy just had five puppies a few weeks ago and every time Jess went by Daisy, she'd jump up to greet her. Daisy has these beautiful brown eyes that just make you melt. She also has these tiny little eyelashes that make her look so sweet. She's a Dachshund mixed with a Beagle. Her coat is reddish brown with hints of white in a few spots. Despite my attempts to woo Jess to the Lab, Daisy won her heart. Since she'd just had her pups we could not adopt her yet. The volunteers told me to keep watching the website to see when she was ready for adoption.

The following Saturday Jessica and I were taking our annual trip to the Erie County Fair. I thought I would surprise her and stop at Pet Connection during their open hours to see Daisy on our way. Well what a trip that was! First the volunteer offered to let us take Daisy for a walk. There is nothing as magical as seeing your daughter's eyes and heart light up as she gets to take a dog for the first walk. When we came back inside the volunteer offered to ask Julie if we could adopt Daisy that day! "Of course," we said. "Yes, please ask her." We were so excited when the volunteer returned and said that Julie gave the OK to adopt Daisy! That was August 22, 2009.

However, we could not bring Daisy home until she weaned her puppies, so we had to wait a few more days for the homecoming. But just knowing she was ours was amazing!

Since joining our family, Daisy has filled our home with love. The volunteers told us that she loves tummy rubs and to this day that has not changed. She also loves to scratch her back on the carpet by twisting and rolling her body on it, a move that we dubbed "The Daisy." I could not picture our family or my home without her. She is truly a treasured member of our family!

— Denise Heineman York

# DASHER

Tonight we celebrated Dasher's fifth birthday. We sang Happy Birthday and gave him a piece of crab cake, his annual birthday treat.

Flash back five years ago when we adopted Dasher (Dash) in December 2012. We were looking for a Terrier mix to replace our Wire Fox Terrier, Asta, who had passed away. A friend of ours who is a Pet Connection volunteer told us to look at the available adoptions online. There was one Terrier mix puppy left with an adorable picture of Dasher wearing a Santa hat. Who could resist that picture?

We filled out the paperwork and were approved to come see Dasher. We remember that day so well. When Julie said "Puppies," a bunch of puppies ran out of the igloo and Dasher was the first pup to run up to us. He poured on his charm and for us it was love at first sight. We brought Dash home the same day and it's been a blessing ever since he became a member of our family.

Dash is intelligent, cuddly, loving and a lap dog. He was very easy to train, too. We taught Dash to ring the bell next to our back door when he wants to go outside. He also gives paw, kisses, knows words and is very perceptive. His favorite thing is to lay on a soft blanket on our lap or lay next to us in a chair. Dasher is all about family and loves when we come home from work. He immediately jumps on our lap waiting for a belly rub. He's very vocal, too. He'll howl when we come home while wagging his tail and jumping up and down. He gets so excited to see us and we're very excited to see him.

He has a girlfriend named Maxine. Maxine is a Dachshund whom Dash met while out on a walk in our neighborhood. It was love at first sight for Dash. He walked up to Maxine and sniffed her face. He then walked away from Maxine, picked up a leaf in his mouth, walked back over to her and dropped it at her front paws. Dash was such a gentleman, it was like a first date. When we ask him if he wants to see Maxine, Dash woofs, wags his tail, runs up on the stairs and gets ready for us to put his leash on to go for a walk.

In January 2017, I was diagnosed with stage three ovarian cancer and underwent two surgeries and six chemo treatments. During that time my body became weak and chemo treatments affected the strength in my legs. Dash sensed I was not doing well, especially when it came to walking. Whenever I was in the hospital for days, Dasher would lay on my recliner for hours, waiting for me to come home. My husband would tell me that Dash looked sad because I wasn't home and did not want to leave my chair. He would lay there for days, only getting up when it was time to eat, drink water, go potty or go for a walk outside.

While recovering from chemo treatments and surgery, Dasher was always by my side watching over me. He would sit outside the bathroom door waiting for me, watch me walk upstairs to make sure I was OK, lay on my lap to provide me comfort or lay at my feet. On the weekends when I experienced pain from my chemo treatment, he would sit on my lap and I would pet him for hours. It helped me to relax and feel loved, knowing how much he cared for me. I'm sure he loved it too, as he would fall asleep on my lap while snoring. Dash has been by my side every step of the way through my recovery. Dasher is a true example of the strong, loving bond between humans and animals.

We are truly blessed to have a dog that loves and cares for us so much. We can't thank Pet Connection enough for all their dedication, love and support they give to the animals at the shelter. We adopted an amazing dog who we believe was meant for us. Our family bond is deeper and stronger with the love from Dasher and we couldn't be happier.

— Mary Hayward

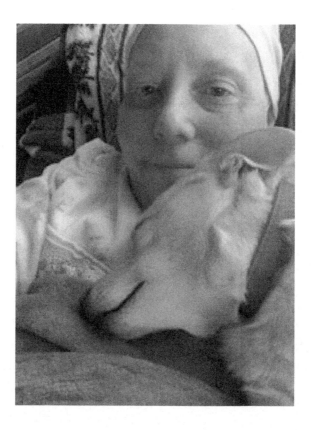

# DEMI

We adopted our dog Demi (Beagle/Jack Russell mix) from Pet Connection in July of 2011. I was doing some volunteer work there at that time and happened to spot this "mama" dog that was just going up for adoption. She had given birth to seven puppies who were now weaned.

As I was parking my car at the shelter, I saw Demi in the yard with the other adult dogs and I called her name. She reluctantly approached the fence to sniff me out and I swear it was love from that point on! Within a few weeks, Demi arrived at her new home in West Seneca. She was a very happy, trusting dog and was great around my young granddaughter as well as the children in the neighborhood.

Demi's demeanor is so sweet and loving that at times I feel as though she knew we had saved her from a horrible fate. I was very interested in finding out more about the history of our beautiful dog. Looking through her paperwork, I found out that Demi originally came from an animal shelter in Menifee County, Kentucky.

After reaching out to them, one of their employees filled me in on

Demi's previous life. She was raised in a quarry with several other dogs that were used for hunting and breeding purposes only. These canines were undernourished, starving, wormy, full of fleas, had to fend for themselves, were endlessly pregnant and living without any type of shelter. How could one not cry after reading this! To think that our beautiful girl was forced to live under these circumstances was just heartbreaking. At least we knew that this would never be part of her life again!

It is truly astounding that animals can be subjected to such extreme conditions and be so loving and sweet when placed in the right type of environment. There are times when we think that Demi has had flashbacks of her previous life but with our love and care, she has overcome many of these horrible memories.

Demi has such a wonderful disposition. She loves her afternoon walks, takes pride in showing off her tricks, enjoys being scratched and thinks nothing about sharing our couch and bed. She approaches anyone who is willing to pay her a bit of attention. This girl has brought us so much joy and we thank Pet Connection every day for this! Life has been very rewarding to both Demi and my family since she came into our lives six years ago!

— Marie Owczarczak

# DOLLY BOO

I had lost my best friend Buster Brown, my eleven-year-old Chihuahua, about three months before I saw the post from Pet Connection of these beautiful Chihuahua Fox Terrier mix puppies and I knew that it was time to find a new friend. We went through the application — all eight pages of it ... ha ha — and went to see these new pups. We fell in love with all of them.

The one that stood out had the biggest mouth and personality of them all. The girls at the shelter jokingly told us, "Just so you know, she's the biggest mouth of them all. You've been warned!"

Dolly Boo, as she has come to be known, has helped me heal and I love her to death. She has helped fill a big hole that I thought would never be filled again. Thank you, Pet Connection, for finding my new baby for us.

— John and Dennis Vogt-Dean

# DUCKY

The decision to add a second dog once again to our family was a no-brainer. After our ten-year-old dog, Jax (a male Golden Retriever) died in the summer of 2014, we knew we would get another companion for our six-year-old male Puggle, Bam. It was just a matter of time, but we were in no rush.

The hardest part was deciding what breed of dog and whether we should get a male or female. We knew we wanted to get a puppy though so that Bam could feel like he was the alpha dog for once ... at least for a little while!

After months slipped by, Christmas was approaching and I started thinking more and more about getting a puppy. I knew about Pet Connection because my sister and my nephew had gotten their dogs there, and they spoke highly of the rescue.

At the end of December I checked their website and there was a picture of the cutest litter of Beagle (or mixed, not sure) puppies and their mom, Jewel. I had two Beagles growing up and it was my late father's favorite breed. I had a feeling one of these was meant to be ours. I emailed Pet Connection immediately and started filling out the application.

At this point, our family decided that we would like a female but Pet Connection could not promise us one or hold one for us. From the pictures on the website, I secretly picked out the cute little Beagle with the pink-speckled nose. I still had some doubts though whether this was the right time for a new addition being that it was in the middle of winter and all, but we forged ahead.

Pet Connection approved our application and the adoption date was to be January 10, 2015. Now that was a definite sign that this was meant to be, at least to me, because this was the date that my dad passed and, like I said, he loved Beagles. My husband and I braved a winter storm that day to go out to Pet Connection. As luck would have it, they had one female still available … the one with the pink-speckled nose! It was love immediately.

While filling out the various papers to get her ready to go home with us, we were informed that her birthday was November 2nd. Another sign that it was meant to be as this is my youngest son's birthday and my sister's birthday, too! One of the girls that was taking care of us asked me if I had a name picked out for her. I did. I told her we decided on "Ducky" after the little dinosaur in "The Land Before Time." We were shocked when she told us that she and others actually talked about how this little girl sometimes looked like a duck. That was the final sign! Ducky was going home.

She is goofy, sweet and loves bunnies! Unfortunately, she lost the pink-speckled nose!

— Joanne Nowak

# DUNCAN

It's a lot of fun having two dogs, watching them play and interact. You get to learn a lot more about dog behavior when you have the privilege to watch them together. I base this on watching Riley and Lily, our two female Labs. When Riley died in November of 2014 I never considered getting another dog until Duncan, formerly Cool Whip, entered the scene.

It was June 2015 when my coworker encouraged me to go down to the lobby of the Larkin Center to see the puppies that Pet Connection was featuring that day. I emailed her back a one-word reply: "Dangerous." I had no idea what breed of dog they would be showcasing and had no intention of getting a puppy. I had just spent six months trying to convince my husband Bob that I was done with getting any more dogs because the pain is so great when they go.

Minutes after we arrived in the lobby I found myself on the floor talking to the puppies through the gate while trying to take pictures on my phone to send to Bob. These were beautiful, white, chubby puppies whose mom was a Great Pyrenees and dad was unknown, which is standard with a Pet Connection puppy.

The puppies weren't up for adoption for two more weeks so it gave me time to convince Bob we needed a second dog. I left the Pet Connection flyer on my dresser so he would have to see the cute puppy faces every time he walked by. I would also mention that they would be on display at a farmers' market in West Seneca. Still, no reaction from him.

Then, on the day they went up for adoption, I came home from work to see a second dog crate in the family room. I freaked out and was so excited! "Is there a puppy in there?" I screamed. Bob calmly said, "Go get our dog." At that moment I emailed Pet Connection with our interest in a puppy. They replied, "Apply only if you are prepared for an 85- to 160-plus-pound dog."

When I called Pet Connection to inquire more about the available puppy they mentioned that the adoption fee would be waived because he was a "swimmer," which was unfamiliar to us. I called our vet right away to find out what it meant but wasn't given a clear explanation. I thought our dreams were dashed because something was seriously wrong with the puppy. Without skipping a beat my husband said, "We're adopting him regardless. He needs a family to love him."

The next morning we went to visit Cool Whip and he reminded me of Bambi on ice. Swimmer puppies have weak muscles in the rear legs and are unable to stand normally as their legs splay out to the side. However, he was bright and playful so we adopted him and named him Duncan!

His first visit to the vet far exceeded our expectations. Dr. Gray knew the condition and presented a very basic solution. All we had to do was hobble the hind legs with white medical tape to make the legs more stable. Within six weeks he was walking normally!

Now Duncan is one and a half years old and weighs one hundred pounds. Once again I get to sit and enjoy the interactions of two dogs in their world. Thank you, Pet Connection, for allowing this beautiful creature into our lives.

— Sue and Bob Dougherty

# ELAINE & MAISIE

I am a nurse by night and a kitty lover by day. One cold, cold night in January, I had a very traumatic night at work. While looking through Facebook trying to forget about my night, I stumbled upon a picture of Elaine and decided to put in an application.

Since moving out of my parent's house, there was an empty hole that my cats used to fill at their house. Later, I went to visit Elaine and fell in love. I thought she'd be a perfect fit for our household.

What I didn't know is that she also had her daughter there. Her name was Ellie, but we renamed her Maisie. Maisie was pregnant at the time so we couldn't adopt them together.

Elaine was happy as a clam at her new forever home, constantly being snuggled and loved. My fiancé and I decided that she should be reunited with her daughter. So, after two months, when Maisie's kittens were able to adopt out, we adopted her as well.

It is crazy to see the amount of love they have for each other. They are always snuggling with each other and running around like crazy women.

We often dress them in Buffalo Bills attire for game day! Go Bills!

Elaine and Maisie fit into our wild life seamlessly. They are there to comfort each other when my fiancé and I work our crazy schedules. I couldn't have asked for a better pet adoption. I love my fur babies!

— Meghan Vandersteur and Michael Palvino

# ELLA

My husband and I were married in 2006 and moved into our own home. We brought along my then nine-year-old cat who previously had lived at my parent's house with another cat. We worked long hours and thought our kitty might be lonely, so after a few months we decided to find her a sibling.

In August 2006, we went to Pet Connection looking for a kitten. There were quite a few kittens there that day. They were all wild and crazy, biting and swatting us, except for one sweet little twelve-week-old girl kitten who was then named Faith. She was sweet and sleepy when we saw her there and my husband fell in love with her. The people at the shelter said she had been dumped in a bag by someone and they weren't even sure she was going to survive when they found her.

Once we got her home we renamed her Ella. It turns out we just happened to find her at a sleepy moment, and she could be quite wild and crazy herself. And, as it also turns out, our older cat had really been OK with being an only child and never really was a huge fan of Ella.

However, Ella is an absolute sweetheart. She loves people and she is patient, snuggly and friendly. Everyone says she's the nicest cat they have ever met.

We called her a "forever kitten" because she is tiny and seemed to have the playful energy of a kitten for many years.

Our first daughter was born when Ella was about three and they have been best friends since day one. Ella lets her do anything and they play together, too! Last year, unfortunately, we lost our older cat, and Ella got two new baby brother kittens. I think Ella would prefer the house without the boy cats, but she has been patient and tolerant with them as well. She is just a love and we are so thankful for her!

— Melissa Laidman

# EMMA

It was late one Sunday evening five years ago when my daughter texted me a picture from college, a lovely little picture of a basket of white Poodle-like puppies up for adoption from Pet Connection. It had been about eight months since our wonderful loving dog of 14 years, Molly, had passed away, and it was heartbreaking. Most of us in the family were ready to welcome a new dog into our house.

Then entered Emma. We did not pick her out, she picked my daughter out. When we were at Pet Connection playing with and holding these adorable little puppies, each would get down and run away, but not this one in particular. She sat at my daughter's knees and did not move. So that was that. In the blink of an eye Emma became a member of our family.

We brought her home that night and she immediately pressed her nose against the sliding glass door and wanted to go potty. This was how well trained she was from Pet Connection; at just a couple of months old she knew what she needed to do to go outside.

This little dog has been our life. Emma has been there through happy times and sad times, always giving us her amazing hugs! The one person in the house that was a little apprehensive of bringing another dog into our lives was my husband. He now refers to Emma as HIS dog. He will look at her and talk to her in a sweet, gentle voice and tell her, "Emma, it's OK, daddy will be right back." It warms my heart to see the love that she has filled his heart with, and all of ours.

Emma is now five years old. She is a quiet dog, but she has a crazy side and it is fun to see her run in circles and crazy eights in the yard. You should see her excitement when she sees her brother return from his home in Colorado and her sister from Pittsburgh. She has a genuinely loving nature about her. Emma definitely cares for people more than dogs but she does tolerate them and has a favorite, Milo, her Dachshund cousin whom she truly enjoys visiting with.

We are more than grateful for Pet Connection! Emma filled a real void in our lives without us even really knowing it. Thank you, Pet Connection, and we love you Emma!

— Lisa Flowers

# EMMA & GEORGE

There is a distinct difference between the smell of life and death, particularly with a dog's acute sense. We came to this realization as we watched our Jack Russell/Beagle mix, Gracie, circle our beloved Lab mix, Molly, who lay too still one cool morning several years ago. Life had to move on as we contemplated Gracie's life without her beloved companion. Of course if we had consulted her, most likely she would have opted to be the top dog of the house. But we didn't.

Eventually this took us to Pet Connection, a maternity shelter out in Marilla. I really appreciate the emphasis this shelter places on moms. We moms need extra care and attention to do what we do. Canine moms are no different.

Lo and behold, we found the perfect little pup. Emma, as she came to be known, was so calm and mild mannered we thought she might be sick. She was simply projecting exemplary puppy behavior because she knew this was her big moment!

We all agreed that this little one-of-a-kind Terrier, Beagle and Dachshund mix was to become part of our forever family. We had just about made a clean escape out the door when something happened that was to change our lives. In trotted this big Hound puppy with big paws, nose, ears and about everything else. He came and plopped himself on my daughter's lap. It took about three milliseconds for this irretrievable thought to go through my head: "Could we get two?" What in the world were we thinking? But there we were driving home with these two lapful's of puppyhood. We now had a pack. Little did Gracie know that her life was about to be turned upside down.

From the get go, George, who by the way grew into this very handsome, 105-pound, 95 percent Rhodesian Ridgeback, appeared to be the biggest weenie there ever was. The day we brought him home he ran and hid beyond the only tree in our back yard when he heard the neighbor's lawnmower start. We thought, "Aww, how endearing!" Well, that "delight" turned into fear aggression. He is the most lovable, loyal, funny boy, but is hostile with other dogs. We also have this strict protocol we follow when new people are introduced. The vigilance is constant and at times is exhausting.

During "Snovember," the snow was as high as our fence in the back yard. The trio decided to simply walk over to the yard of our neighbor. Not good. George panicked because he was out of his comfort zone and did not have the best encounter with our very tolerant, dog-loving neighbor. Recently, we were out walking the pack (on leashes), minding our own business when a dog got loose and charged in. In seconds, George had the dog pinned down, my husband was down, and next thing I knew, there was blood everywhere. The stranger dog had a hold of my husband's hand and wouldn't let go. George was simply trying to protect his alpha.

All this said, it has not been easy. However, I am from the school of thought that when you adopt an animal, you're in it for the long haul. You commit to the inconveniences and issues, with the exception of extreme circumstances. George has been a real challenge in unconditional love, one that we wish others would take as seriously when considering the big decision of adding a pet to the family. When the day comes that George leaves this earth, we perhaps will breathe a sigh of relief, but he will leave a huge hole in our hearts.

— Sue Giovino

# FRED

My husband and I adopted this little guy in February of 2017 and he has been a very good pup!

Fred and our Shepherd wrestle all day and chase each other around the yard. They are never far from each other. He also loves to go on walks and go camping and swimming. He is very smart and learns quickly. He is also a bed hog!

It makes us feel good that we are able to give Fred a good life, especially since he had such a rough start being abandoned in a field. After all, they are only here for a short while and they deserve the best we can give them.

— Pamela Steger

# GILLIGAN

We are a dog family! I've had a dog my whole life and when I married Mike, thank goodness he was a dog lover, too.

We had just lost one of our dogs, Finster. We still had other dogs at home but there was a bit of a void. My cousin and her son had volunteered at Pet Connection so I began following them on Facebook. A post of a mom, Dixie, came across my news feed. I followed the story and the birth of her puppies. I then filled out the application and we were accepted.

There were some concerns. We were a "big dog" family and have never owned a smaller dog. However, we felt that this little guy would be a good fit.

Luke, our son, had already picked out the one we wanted online. We were number two for adoption so there was a pretty good chance we were going to get the one we wanted. He and I went to pick out our puppy. The puppies were playing and goofing around when a staff member said, "That little tan one is the bully of the litter." That was all we needed to hear as we figured he'd fit right in with our crazy clan.

We named him Gilligan figuring he'd be everyone's little buddy. Gilligan is all personality. He is friendly, full of energy and is a nonstop bundle of fun. He also has a softer side and cuddles up to you the moment you sit down. He fits in great with our other dogs. He's a big dog in a little dog's body. He has the best personality and his name truly fits him — he's everyone's little buddy!

He completes our dog clan, who we affectionately call "The Fab Five."

— Lisa Blas

# GUENTHER

Losing my beloved Casey, a rescued Irish Wolfhound, in August of 2008 was devastating. He was the rock that helped me navigate the uncharted seas of being widowed at the early age of 57. Days that followed were empty and unfulfilled. I sleepwalked through each day, made the right responses but fooled no one.

After the last vestiges of Christmas were boxed and the last cookie eaten, my daughter Susan began campaigning to find me a new companion and in the process, ironically, added to her own family of hounds with a six-year-old Lab named Hannah. There were countless weekend trips to shelters and on May 30, 2009, I stood before Pet Connection and was admitted ten minutes before the official opening time. That ten minutes played a major part in my happy union!

When Susan related my meeting of Guenther to her brother, Marc, she described it as, "Mom leaped over baby gates like an Olympic sprinter!" I saw a grey bundle of thick fur, big brown eyes and love. I wasn't familiar with the breed, Norwegian Elk Hound, and didn't even check gender. I just clutched him likely a Black Friday shopper getting a Vizio TV for $59.99!

The ten minutes come into play as I was completing the adoption papers and two families came in for a second look at the male Elk Hound! A baby book of Norse names provided Guenther's regal handle. From that glorious day on, my clothes have been covered in black, grey and white strands of hair and my credit card gets maxed out at Clyde's Feed store. Guenther had private lessons at obedience school and sleeps in his own room on a crib-sized mattress. He cheers Norway during the Winter Olympics wearing a hand-knit sweater. He enjoys steel-cut oatmeal and $30 Bully Sticks.

I didn't adopt or rescue. I am in a committed relationship. We cuddle together every night and I tell him how brave and handsome he is and never bring up his fear of vacuums and stink bugs. I have published poetry about Guenther and he has a fan club who share their doggie bag treats.

My bumper sticker won't tell you who I voted for but honestly states, "I found my Prince Charming at the Pet Connection and he has four feet and sharp canines." I don't take this unconditional love for granted and wake up each morning knowing a delightful, delicious wet kiss is waiting!

## Ode To Guenther

*My Dockers have no laces*
*My underwear is torn*
*There are holes in a blanket*
*I've had since I was born.*
*I wade through shredded paper*
*I'm not showered and uncombed*
*I don't have some strange malady*
*But a new puppy in my home.*

— Carol Thrun Nowicki

# GUS

Last summer, my family and I had to say goodbye to our twelve-year-old beloved Golden Retriever, Sunny. She left a hole in our hearts and we never thought we'd get over her passing.

My father-in-law, Chief, is a volunteer at Pet Connection and told me about the recent birth of pups. I was reluctant at first to even think about getting another dog so close after my Sunny girl had passed, but I looked through the photos anyway.

Almost immediately I fell in love with the sweet, chubby, black puppy with the four white paws. I felt an instant connection with him even though we never met in person! Strange how their photos tug at your heartstrings.

I asked my father-in-law about "white paws" and it turns out he was a secret favorite of his as well! So, we began the process of adoption. Once we were granted, we went to (hopefully) go get our "white paws" at our appointment at Pet Connection.

Well, he was still there as if it was meant to be! My children were so thrilled. I cried, and my husband (who's a very large, tough guy) spoke to our new puppy in baby talk!

Today, May 25th, is Sweet Gus' first birthday and we are celebrating his gentle soul. He's a Lab, Collie and Shepherd mix, super smart, very obedient and very good at snuggling. He loves chewing on stuff that isn't his, eats the crotch out of any underwear left on the floor, dives into the bathroom garbage can, chases the cat all day long, bites on poor Rain's ears (our four-year-old Lab who actually enjoys her brother's wrestling), digs out any newly planted bushes in the yard and is an all-around pain-in-the-butt puppy. But, he's a loving gentle giant, has one ear larger than the other, enjoys laying on top of you on the couch, follows me around the house within two feet at all times, has paws the size of dinner plates and gives kisses to anyone that he doesn't frighten with his very loud bark. And he loves the sprinkler.

He is the best rescue pup we could have wished for and been blessed with. He filled a void in our hearts when Sunny left us. Every day is an adventure, and sweet Gus lives up to his name!

With love and wet puppy kisses …

— The Miller Family

# HAZEL

In January 1995, The Buffalo News ran "Pet Project: Ox the dog needs a friend." An eight-week-old Boxer-Shepherd attracts my eye. My wife agrees, we can get a dog!

I drove out to Pet Connection with excitement. The litter of six was running loose in the kitchen and they were all biding for my attention, but one persevered. I made arrangements to adopt the cutest, smartest little puppy of the bunch, soon to be named Hazel, and plopped her on the front seat of my car.

As we made the thirty-mile trip back to Buffalo, I could already tell she was special. There she sat in full attention on the front seat for the whole ride back, never making a peep, just as excited as I to be on a new adventure.

We owned a shoe store in Buffalo at the time and I brought her to the store that day where she would "work" side by side with me for the next six years. She became a popular fixture on the Elmwood strip — she even had her own celebrity column in Artvoice! She would hang out in front where regulars would come by to play catch with her or maybe go down the street to Mr. Goodbar to have a beer with Charlie or do some dumpster diving with her friend Richie. She was always getting herself into trouble.

One morning she went missing from our front yard on the lower West Side of Buffalo; someone had taken her. We were devastated. We scoured the neighborhood for the next three days looking for her. We came across horrible things while looking for her but we got a tip (for $100) that she had been taken by a dog fighting ring. It was raided the next day by the Buffalo Police and the Buffalo Pound. There was no one there as they had been tipped off.

We knew one of the policemen who was at the raid and told him what happened. He said he would take care of it. Word on the street was, "If the dog didn't show up, people were going to jail." Hazel was found in the parking lot of the pound that same evening. The pound didn't realize from our lost dog flyer that it was her. The next morning we were crying that we would never see her again and my wife said, "Let's just go down there to look." To our surprise, there she was.

Hazel lived another happy twelve years and was a month shy of fifteen when she passed. She loved to play Frisbee, swim in the lake or go to John's Deli to eat scraps off the floor. She would sometimes run alongside my bike the two miles to get to work. She was a beast. She played Frisbee the day before she died. We loved Hazel. Thanks, Pet Connection, for a great dog.

— Bob Kotas

# HENRY

I met Henry while volunteering at Pet Connection. His spunky personality and unique markings caught my eye from the start. Our yellow Lab Gunther was four at the time, and I decided it would be nice to adopt a rescue so Gunther could have a little brother.

Henry is a Border Collie/Spaniel with possibly some Cattle Dog and Blue Tick Hound in the mix. I soon found out that herders and retrievers are like night and day!

When Henry met Gunther, he adored him from the start; he herded him and snuggled with him every chance he got. Not only does Henry take Gunther's squeaky toys, but if Gunther doesn't respond he goes one step further by squeaking them on Gunther's head or belly. Luckily, Gunther is laid back and tolerant and has accepted that having a little brother can be annoying at times.

As a pup, Henry regularly visited a classroom of elementary students with special needs. On one occasion, I received a thank you from the teacher. She had watched with emotion as a distraught first grader laid on the floor with Henry's paw on his arm, and told him all about what was troubling him. It's amazing how animals are able to connect with us without saying a word.

Henry is now going on four years old. He and his older brother Gunther continue to make us laugh and smile. They are an important part of our family.

— Jill Keller

# JACK

After much encouragement from our adult children, my husband and I decided to explore the possibility of adopting a rescue companion for our two-year-old black Lab. At least I "thought" that's what we were doing. Three of us had volunteered at Pet Connection Programs Inc., so we knew we'd be adopting from them. We had done everything from bathing and grooming new rescues to socializing puppies and lending a hand on adoption days, and we were familiar with their adoption process.

Having religiously watched Pet Connection's Facebook posts highlighting new adoption-ready litters, we saw a puppy that we were interested in meeting. I filled out and submitted the application and was approved; adoption day finally arrived! My husband had an unexpected meeting to attend and was unable to join me at the shelter. Apparently his last words to me as he hurried out the door were, "If you find one you like, call me and I'll leave the meeting and join you there."

Later that day I placed a blanket-lined box into my car and brought a small towel with me to pick up the scent of the litter "in case" I decided to adopt one. I thought it might help the pup not feel so lonely in his crate at night if he could snuggle in with the familiar scent of his litter mates. I had my heart set on the male tri-colored Australian Shepherd mix and to my delight he was still there! But, looks aren't everything, so I spent a good amount of time playing with him and watching him interact with his siblings.

As with all things "meant to be," I fell in love. I finished the adoption process, tucked that little fluff ball into my car and headed home. As soon as I pulled into the driveway I texted a picture of him to my husband with the message, "I got the fluffy one!"

His reaction to my text reminded me that I had skipped an important step in the adoption process — confirming with the hubby! Luckily I married a good-natured man who now has a great story to tell about how we came to adopt our Jack.

Jack is now a well-adjusted two-year-old Aussie mix and is best friends with his Lab sister Maggie. I admit to having had some serious "adopter's regret" in those early months of training. Jack is a high-energy, highly reactive dog. We have worked hard and even enlisted a trainer to get him adjusted to our home and lifestyle. He's now our Velcro dog — always attached to one of us — after his energy is expended! He is ever alert, which can be a bit much with the presence of wildlife in our rural backyard. He keeps us all moving, whether it's taking walks, playing fetch or retrieving toys from under the sofa.

We are grateful to Pet Connection for the good work they do. And Jack, we are so glad we found you!

— Susan Vail Bach

# JAX & ELLIE

This is Jax and Ellie — formerly Fred and Wilma — on their first night in their fur-ever home. They are much bigger now, but this still is my favorite picture of them cuddled up with my son Kamrin.

Jax is the vocal one and likes to make his presence known quite frequently. Ellie, however, is a little princess who chose my husband as her favorite human.

They have added quite a bit of excitement to our family. I am so glad we decided to adopt them. Their big brother Sam (our dog) even loves them, even though they enjoy ganging up on him. Together they are the Samuel "Elle" Jackson crew and we just love them all so much!

— Kim Newland

# JESSICA

The day I saw the picture of Jessica I knew I needed her in my life. After years of hopelessly begging my mom for a dog, I figured I'd get a no, but I asked anyways.

Jessica didn't just need a family, she deserved a family. When the application went through I checked my email every two minutes waiting for a reply, and as soon as I had that I went to meet Jessica as soon as possible. I made my family drop all of their plans (as this should be the upmost important day for all of them).

The moment I saw Jessica I was immediately in tears with so many emotions running through my head. If heaven was somewhere on earth, I think it would be the moment she came into my life. Now Jessica is my best friend, travel buddy and peace of mind after a long day. She was worth the wait.

Coming into our home, Jessica weighed 120 pounds and the vet told us she needed to lose at least thirty pounds to be at a healthy weight. Due to that diagnosis, she and I both went on a diet and started walking, and eventually running, as I began training for 5Ks. We pushed and motivated each other to be the healthiest and happiest we've ever been.

I am glad to say that since she has been with us she has dropped a lot of weight and gained a lot of energy. Now we enjoy nice long walks at night, visiting my great grandma and snuggling up to end our day. I couldn't imagine my life without our big fur baby and I am so thankful for the opportunity to give her a forever home.

— MacKenzie Holla

# KOURTNEY

We've adopted three cats from Pet Connection, and I now volunteer there. We are a cat-loving family and our story is about one of the cats. Her name is Kourtney and she is now eight years old.

On an evening four years ago when I was volunteering, sitting on the floor trying to get a very scared cat named Mickey out of a cage, a small cat that I had never seen before approached me and simply sat on my lap. She then put her paws on my chest and started rubbing her chin on mine! All this time the cat in the cage growled at the cat on my lap, but she paid no attention.

The very next week, again I was on the floor and this time I was able to get the scared cat out of his cage. Kourtney again came up to me and did the very same thing that she did a week earlier. I asked another volunteer who this cat was. I was told that her nickname was "Scaredy Cat" because only one other volunteer could approach her. She ran from everyone else. She was adopted out but returned when all she did was hide in a hole in a wall.

I decided to adopt her the very next week. For awhile she wouldn't come out of our basement. Fast forward to today and she gets along very well with our other four cats. She sleeps with us at night. She is very approachable and so very lovable. I am so happy that she adopted me!

— Carol Sporysz

# LIBBEY

We adopted Libbey in 2006. My husband had just returned from a tour in Kuwait and he had been gone for 8-1/2 months. He was a member of the Navy Seabees and served in Operation Desert Storm.

My daughter was on the Pet Connection website looking at dogs that were up for adoption and just fell in love with Libbey's face. Her story was typical of many that have come through your doors. She was rescued with a litter of puppies from a mill in Ohio. The puppies had all been adopted by the time our daughter first saw her. When we came out as a family to meet Libbey, she was very afraid of everything. She was not trusting of my husband at all at first. We took her for a short walk around your property and knew that we needed to give her a loving forever home.

It took almost four years to completely housebreak her. A lot of love, patience and trust went into her but she is a good dog. She has slowed over the years as she is now around 12-1/2 years old.

Thank you for taking her in years ago so that she could end up living a life of leisure and become a member of our family.

— The Sims Family

# LILY

I first saw Lily (formerly Razzle) when I was volunteering at Pet Connection in 2009. She was with her two brothers, all about twelve weeks old. They were all very shy and afraid. I could have socialized the other younger pups there, but I wanted to work with these shy pups.

What a difference a few hours of love and attention made. In the beginning, Lily and her brothers, so shy and scared, would not come near me and would run away when approached. However, after quietly sitting with these three pups for a long time, one at a time they slowly and carefully approached me. I talked to them, played with them and pet them. Suddenly, they couldn't get enough petting and attention. They craved it.

I immediately fell in love with all three of them, but knew I wanted to adopt Lily as soon as possible. I left work early the day the pups went up for adoption to take her home and made sure I was the first person there, on time! My husband and I adopted Lily in September of 2009.

Today, she loves going for walks and running, playing ball outside, going to her grandparent's house to play with their dog Sam (also from

Pet Connection) and opening up a BarkBox full of toys and treats every month.

Lily sleeps in a warm, comfy bed and enjoys being pet and snuggling on the couch. She follows us everywhere and is always at my feet. She just celebrated her eighth birthday and is still a happy little pup at heart. Lily is the best dog we have ever owned and we love her so much. Thank you Pet Connection!

— Laura Witkowski

# LOLA

I already had two cats and one miniature Pinscher/Chihuahua mix named Elliott, but something made me casually search the shelter animals in the area. I came across Lola.

Although I continued to look through all the wonderful animals in need of a home, I kept going back to Lola. Her story seemed to connect with me. The new mom was described as very shy with people but great with all dogs. She had been at the shelter for at least five months and they were worried she may never find her forever home. I was up for a challenge and knew that as long as she was OK with Elliott — which it sounded like she would be — then she would have a forever home despite how she was with the humans in her life.

When I first saw Lola at the end of summer 2012, she hid behind her caretaker at the shelter and stared at me. I knew she would be OK. She had formed a bond with the caretaker and she was interested in people. She was terrified of the ride home but really enjoyed playing with Elliott when she met him. Elliott was very happy, too.

Over the next few months, Lola made adjustments slowly. When she went out to the back yard, she was cautious about running by any human in order to get in or out of the house. I had to open the door, walk away and wait for her to exit or enter. Eventually she realized that she was safe and now practically runs over my feet to get in or out of the house. She also would not let anyone touch her. She took over a chair in the living room and every time I walked by I got closer and closer, inch by inch, no eye contact, then sideways glances until one day I was able to touch her! That was the most exciting day up to that point. Now, four years later, I even know her tickle spots and can tell that she loves to be loved.

As I mentioned earlier, Lola claimed a chair in the living room. She slept there all the time, even as the other animals slept with me. She was an anxious little one and I could hear her pace at night. I would spray lavender and she would go back to her chair and sleep.

One day, the night before Thanksgiving, I noticed her checking out the bed while I was in a different room nearby. I was quiet. She did not stay, but slept another night on her chair. The next morning, Thanksgiving, I woke up and had my Thanksgiving miracle. There, jumping onto the bed and walking straight for me was my Lola. At that moment, I knew that she was choosing to be loved and that she was confident that all this good stuff was for real. Now, most nights she beats me to bed and every night she curls up next to me.

I credit much of Lola's transformation to Elliott. Throughout everything, she followed his lead. As he gave hugs, she watched. As he was leashed up, she watched and demanded to go wherever he was going. She has brought so much joy to the house and I could never imagine her being put down and not being around. She wakes up every morning jumping like a reindeer as if to say she is happy it is another new day. She loves to go for walks and cannot stop smiling. She expresses her happiness via her whole shaking body and she makes everyone around her so happy.

— Denise Staffa

# LOVER & SISSY

Several years ago I did some volunteer work for Pet Connection Programs Inc. Whenever I walked into the shelter, one of the kittens that was caged by the door would reach out and gently touch me on my cheek. It was so tender and loving that I had to adopt him. I named him Lover because he was so affectionate.

Of course, I could not separate him from his sister so I adopted her as well and named her Sissy. Ten years later and still in love! They curl up on their lounge chair every afternoon to assist in bathing one another and then settle in for a nap (one of many). Love my babies ...

The yellow cat is Lover, and the gray is Sissy.

— Lynne Day

# LUKE

I always said when I moved into my own house I was going to get a dog. We had a Beagle several years before, but when his time came it was too difficult to think about getting another dog.

So, many years later when I finally moved out and got my own place, one of the first things I wanted to do was get a dog. I had been living there for a year or so, looking every now and then for a dog. My friends would let me know when they saw some listed in the paper or online, but none of them were the one I was looking for.

Then a friend sent me a link to the Pet Connection website and they had just listed a litter of Beagle puppies. There were five in the litter, all males, and they would be up for adoption on a Saturday. The pictures of them were adorable and I had to go see them in person.

I asked my parents if they would come along with me and off we went. We got there early in the afternoon and were welcomed into the house to see the puppies. Now, one had already been adopted and another was in the hands of another family that was there, so there were three little guys left. One was sleeping under the table on a pillow, one was chewing on the shoelaces of the volunteer that was working there, and then there was the last little guy. He came right up to the little fence, jumped up and started licking my face. That was it. This was the one. I didn't pick him out, he picked me out.

He was the cutest little puppy I'd ever seen, and I still think so to this day. I paid the adoption fee, was given some supplies and home we went. I'm just glad that my folks came along as I really didn't think I'd be going home with him right then and there, and he was a little wiggle worm all the way home!

When I got him he was just black and white, but as the weeks went by he started to get the brown fur too, and he's been a great little guy ever since. When the first snow came, he wasn't quite sure what to make of it; he took one step outside, touched the snow and decided nope, I don't like this, and went right back into the house! He's since changed his tune on the snow and loves to go jumping around in it. He still doesn't like the rain though.

He loves to snuggle and will jump up and cuddle up no matter where you sit. He follows me around everywhere and I wouldn't have it any other way. Luke has been the best thing that has happened to me.

— Mike Chlebowy

# LUNA

Our Pet Connection story begins with the passing of my mother, a dog lover through and through. Shortly after she lost her battle with cancer, my sisters and I wondered if we shouldn't look to find my dad a furry little friend to help keep him company.

After looking around online, I went out to Pet Connection to meet a nice girl named Greta who recently had puppies and would soon be available. I thought she'd be a perfect companion and was ready to adopt her on behalf of my dad, but Pet Connection wisely made us make sure that dad was definitely on board with such a commitment. And understandably so, since Pet Connection was only doing their best to ensure Greta's next move would be to her fur-ever home.

Unfortunately, my dad just wasn't ready. After explaining this to my wife, she opened the door for me slightly by saying, "Well, what about Greta for us?" I quickly burst right through that opening, but by the time I got back into contact with Pet Connection about Greta, she had already been adopted to the very next lucky family that came to meet her.

We looked around for another potential adoption for my family, but nothing seemed promising until we came back to Pet Connection to meet a nice new mom dog named Luna. She was a bit nervous and skittish, but I could tell she was a very sweet girl. And shortly thereafter, we brought Luna to her new fur-ever home in Lockport.

After only a few days it felt like Luna had been a part of our family for years. She has now developed into a great guard dog and she always keeps a keen eye on the whereabouts of our UPS truck driver. When the kids are playing in the yard, any bumps, bruises and/or crocodile tears are quickly licked away by immediate doggy kisses to the affected area.

The best part of our story is, several weeks after Luna's adoption, as I was looking through Luna's adoption paperwork, I noticed that her birthday was listed as January 8th. That happens to be the same day we lost my mom to cancer.

A coincidence? Perhaps ... but if you actually do the math and divide one by 365, there is a less than 0.003 percent chance of this actually being so.

I like to think that my mom had an awful lot to do with my family getting to adopt our sweet girl Luna, and I know mom would have just adored her.

We can't thank Pet Connection enough for our loyal family member.

— The Radwanski Family

# LUNA & NULA

In 2012, my daughter Lea was scanning the web for a small dog to be her companion while she was away at graduate school. She was studying to be an optometrist and living alone was lonely. She spotted the Pet Connection website and immediately fell in love with four little black-and-white Shih Tzu/Chihuahua pups. We filled out the paperwork and, happily, she was approved to adopt a pup.

Unfortunately, Lea was stuck in Chicago so I went to select her dog. She requested one of the fluffy, long-haired pups. There were two with long hair and two with short hair, all females weighing a mere two to four pounds.

When I arrived at the site to choose a pet I immediately noticed the largest pup (short hair) just running around. She looked like she would be a handful, getting into everything and teasing the others. That left just three, and I selected the smallest of the dogs even though she had short hair because she just laid on the floor taking the abuse from her larger sister. I felt I was saving her from future torment, and the ease of maintenance of the coat for a busy student was a bonus.

Lea, not upset with my choice, named her Luna. They spent the rest of the summer at home and everyone fell in love with the puppy.

A couple of days after Luna's arrival home I realized that I would miss this little cutie. (I had a police K-9 German Shepherd, my partner Herc.) I called Pet Connection and asked if I could take another pup. The woman on the phone said yes and asked which one. I told her I didn't care. She quickly said, "I will put the other short-haired pup aside for you."

Ha, I was getting the instigator! I picked up Luna's sister and named her Nula. They were reunited and enjoyed each other's company. And, Luna soon became capable of defending herself. Luna weighs 10 pounds while Nula weighs 14 pounds.

Nula was and is a very active dog. Her favorite game was jumping all around Herc and playing with him. She loved stealing his huge bones. They were best of friends. We walked every day together. Herc and I retired two years ago and he passed away in the fall from cancer. I felt so sorry for Nula as she looked lost wondering where her bud went.

Luna visits often from Cleveland and the dogs enjoy playing together. Both dogs have brought so much happiness to everyone. Adopting from Pet Connection was a great experience and I am a supporter. The shelter truly does amazing work. Thank you!

— Mary Ellen Sawicki

# MAGGIE

A little over eight years ago I was living with my fiancée and my two children who were seven and ten at the time. They always had a dog in their young lives and had been asking if we could get another one.

I found Pet Connection through an internet search and decided to take a drive there. We told the children we were going on a nice drive in the country. Upon arriving, they were onto us. The volunteers brought out dogs one at a time to see how they — and we — reacted.

The third dog that was brought out was Noel, and she had given birth to her pups on Christmas Eve 2008. She wouldn't stop wagging her tail and kissing my children.

We adopted her immediately. It was April 11, 2009. The next day we attended church for Easter, leaving her alone. When we returned she was still on the couch and happy to see us. No damage! We renamed her

Maggie and to this day she is the most loving and well-behaved dog we've known.

— Paul Hoock and Family

# MAX

We had to put down our previous dog due to complications from diabetes. It was a sad weekend. My husband and I looked for a place open on Sunday to adopt another puppy to surprise our sons, but to no avail.

Early Monday morning I checked Pet Connection's website and found two litters up for adoption that afternoon at 4 p.m. My youngest son sent photos of the puppies to my husband and older son to choose a puppy that we could adopt. We all chose the same one!

We were the first to arrive for adoptions so we got to pick first. When the man opened the door to the kennel area, the puppy we all picked was the first one to run up to my son! We knew it was a match made in heaven.

I filled out all the paperwork and was approved. I thought we would have to come back for the little guy but they said, "He can go home with you today." I was not prepared! My son called his brother and told him to go to the pet store and buy a collar and leash because a new family member was on his way home with us.

Our Max turned eight on June 8th, and we couldn't have found a better dog anywhere! He has a quirky personality, is very affectionate, very playful, follows basic commands (when he wants to), has a toy box of his own and is spoiled rotten. He now has an Alaskan Malamute sister who is seven. We got her as a puppy when Max was one and they get along great.

Max will "sing" for you if you ask him, and he likes singing to the fire engines when he hears them. He makes us laugh every day and is always there to greet you at the door with a toy in his mouth, ready to play!

Thank you, Pet Connection!

— Amy Kline

# MAX

This is the story of Max, formerly known as Kojac, from Pet Connection. We adopted Max back in March of 2007. I was searching online for a puppy as I had lost my "heart" dog, Taz, in December of 2006 and I needed to have the love of a dog in my life again. I found pictures on their website and I was immediately in love with Max's little face.

My husband did not want another dog just yet, but as fate would have it, Taz's dog license renewal had come in the mail the very day that the pups were going up for adoption. It was a sign. I cried my eyes out and begged my husband to just go look at the puppies. Well, it worked. We drove over to the rescue and out in the yard, all alone on a hill of dirt covered with a tarp was my boy. I went right to him, picked him up and never put him down. He was sick with a cold but I knew I could nurse him back to health and I did.

Max became my best friend. I taught him everything and he was a smart boy. He was part German Shepherd so he would spend hours out in the yard just "watching" and I would sit with him and we would just watch. He loved the snow and would sit outside right in the snow as if it wasn't even there. My husband once built a snowman which had a carrot for a nose — bad idea. Max ate his nose!

He loved to go for walks and he would find a stick to carry in his mouth and would carry it with him the entire time. I still have one of his sticks! He was such a good boy.

Max became ill in 2009 and ended up having Addison's disease. I was so scared at first; there was no way I could lose my boy! We got him on meds and faithfully took him to the vet every four weeks for his shot. He did great — he was such a trooper. He loved going to the vet because they gave him treats and he loved food! Max was definitely a "foodie."

In March of 2015, Max became ill again. He was bleeding internally, most likely from the years of meds that he had to be on, but he had to be on them or he wouldn't have survived. On March 16, 2015, we had to make the hardest decision of our lives. There was nothing that could be done to stop the bleeding and believe me, I would have done anything! We had to let Max go at the young age of eight. It was so sudden.

I loved that boy with all of my heart and soul, and he was the best dog I have ever had. I would not change one single thing about my time with him and I am so grateful to Pet Connection for giving him his chance at life. He had a wonderful life, and as it turns out, Max was my "heart" dog. I will miss him for the rest of my life.

— Darlene Hippert

# MILEY

Back in March of 2013, my family and I decided we would like a puppy. We were not sure where we were going to go, but we knew we wanted to adopt. We came across the Pet Connection Programs Inc. website and just fell in love with the photos of Luna and her puppies.

I filled out the application and patiently waited for the phone call to let us know if we were approved or not. The day the call came was the best day ever!

When we arrived for our appointment, the ladies that were working were great. They were very friendly and helpful with all the questions that we had. The puppy we chose was sleeping at the bottom of the bunch, and I told my daughter we needed to see what she was all about. She was so tiny, only weighing about six pounds. One of the ladies had picked her up and taken her outside for us. After a couple of minutes of walking around she crawled into my purse. I knew right then and there she was going home with us!

We named her Miley and she has been the greatest addition to our family. She is beyond spoiled and we could not imagine our lives without her. She loves to cuddle, go for walks, stalk the squirrels and gives high-fives when we ask her!

Thank you so much for the amazing job that you do with the moms and puppies, as well as the kittens that you take care of. Making sure that they go to a trusting family is awesome.

— The Vanderburgh Family

# MILLER

On August 29, 2005, Hurricane Katrina hit the Gulf Coast devastating New Orleans and displacing millions of people and God only knows how many of our four-legged fur babies. My family watched it on the news as not a single channel was not covering this historic storm.

People's lives were changed, and so was ours. My husband had been diagnosed with a blood immune disorder and we were in for a rough ride with it. Nothing ever went right with his treatments and he had so many side effects. Christmas rolled around and two days later our beloved German Shepherd Rusty suddenly passed away. I was devastated. I adopted him from a local shelter and he was my rock.

My children were older but saw that mom wasn't mom without a dog. My son searched the internet and found a puppy on the Pet Connection website, but we were broke. Medical bills and medications took a priority. But, we had a huge change collection, started counting it up, cashed it in and drove out to Marilla.

We were greeted by many cats on the premises and were told to check our vehicle before we leave in case a stowaway was found. We went in this old house and were greeted by the staff who directed us to the puppies my son found. I opened the door to the puppy room and one ran out so I chased him down and carried him back.

In the room were six fuzzy black bundles jumping for attention or attempting to escape the room again. My daughter was in the room trying to quickly pay attention to them. I came back with the runaway and she's says, "Hey mom, look at this one." There was a puppy just laying there gently tugging on her pant leg. He wasn't jumping or trying to run away, so I picked up this fur ball, took him by the window and start crying. I truly missed my other dog.

My daughter was like, "Mom, it's OK. Let's take him."

We went back to the staff with puppy in arms and filled out the required paperwork. One of the workers looked over and said don't be surprised if he barks with a southern drawl. We were all puzzled and asked what he meant. He said these were Katrina puppies from New Orleans, and our jaws hit the ground. We are doing a good thing by taking this puppy home because his home and people were probably gone.

We named him Miller after Ryan Miller of the Buffalo Sabres. He has always been a good dog. Even as a puppy he was pretty mellow. He's twelve now and his hips are arthritic, but we've built him a ramp and assist him with getting around. He loves cheeseburgers and mashed potatoes.

— Lori Hamann

# MISSY & PANDA

In August 2016 I started following Pet Connection on Facebook after a friend of mine had shared one of their posts. My husband and I had talked about eventually getting a small dog when we had a house of our own. However, since we were still living with family we decided it was not the right time to look for a dog.

As the days went on, I began to see pictures of two dogs on the Pet Connection page, Missy and Panda. I could not stop looking at the pictures as Panda looked very much like our family dog, Cookie, who we had to put down in September 2015.

I began reading comments on their pictures from people praying for the two bonded dogs to find a home together. They had been at Pet Connection since July when they were found and had their puppies. I would show their pictures to my husband and mother, but kept talking myself out of adopting them since we were not yet in a house and had never had two dogs at the same time before.

Eventually, we decided to fill out the application and make an appointment to meet them. When we walked into the building on October 1, 2016 and saw them, there was no way we could leave without them. We brought them home and have been in love ever since.

Over the past year Missy and Panda have both gotten used to life with us and their true personalities now show. Panda is a little crazy at times, but loves to be with people and to give kisses and cuddles. Missy was a bit reserved at first but has definitely opened up and has become more affectionate. My husband and I recently bought our first home and were nervous as to how they would adjust, but it could not have gone better! We find them sleeping on the couch or bed and laying down looking out the windows. They definitely love to lay out in the sun on our deck and run around their new yard and chase the bunnies!

Adopting Missy and Panda was the best decision we made and we cannot imagine our life or family without them!

— Lauren Burton

# MR. FRITZ

In 2007, after a life-changing accident, I was feeling very depressed about being in a wheelchair and relearning to walk was going slow, but the hardest part was the loneliness I felt. On October 10, 2011, I was introduced to my new best friend. He was a rolly-polly, black-and-brown Patterdale Terrier mix named Mr. Fritz. We bonded right away and the black clouds above me started to disappear.

Mr. Fritz and I went through special training together so he could learn to walk safely with me and my walker. He also learned sign language and how to help me.

Today you can find him playing fetch outside (his favorite activity), playing with the children (he is awesome with kids) or sleeping on the hassock that my feet rest on. I don't know where I would be today without his love and help.

People tell me I did a wonderful thing by rescuing him, but I think that he is the one that rescued me. Thank you, Pet Connection, for giving me my life back!

— Audrey L. Sharp

# NORMA JEAN MARIE

All of our pets are rescues, and the latest is little Norma Jean Marie. She had been through more than any two-year-old cat should have to endure when she was dumped at the door of Pet Connection. She was neutered and brought back to health there and offered for adoption to a quiet home due to her past brutal experiences.

We were fortunate to welcome her home with us to join our two older cats, Boo Boo Marie and Shelly Marie, and our fourteen-year-old parakeet Shark Boy.

She decided our bed was her bed on the second day, chose to use the family litter box instead of her own, and knew to wait in line to be fed last as the pecking order defined. And she started to run and play, involving the other cats who thought their quiet laying in front of the heat vents days were the previous goal. Soccer with toys and balls were best played with at least one other cat and usually at night! When she "catches" a toy mouse or bird, she proudly meows with it in her mouth and puts it slimily down in front of you. She gets extra rubs for being such a good hunter.

Lap sitting and pillow sleeping, at her request, are supplied as needed.

She has brought so much happiness to all of us. Thank you, Pet Connection, for being there for her and so many others.

— Sally Kutter

# PARKER

We adopted a puppy in January 2009, shortly after buying our first home. This puppy was so adorable we could not say no. We took our daughter, who at the time was twelve years old, with us and surprised her.

She and my husband had always wanted a dog, but as renters it wasn't a good idea. It was the ideal time to add a new member to our family. We had many discussions on our way home about what we would name the puppy and as we passed a street near our home, the street name became the puppy's name — Parker.

This dog has brought us so much joy and laughter. We were told that he was the runt of the litter and may be a bit skittish as he got older. I truly have no idea how they can predict his behavior so young. He is the most loving dog ever. My grandkids adore him.

When he was a puppy and we had a cage for him, my two-year-old granddaughter and the puppy would take turns in the cage. My grand-daughter would literally lock herself in the cage and the dog out of it. The dog would sit outside the cage and cry like a baby to get back in. We would make my granddaughter get out so that the puppy could get back in his bed, and she would then be on the outside crying to get back in. It was kind of crazy, but funny, too.

That granddaughter and this dog became so close. She could do just about anything to this dog and he would allow it. But he has this thing about going for walks — he is against it completely! We live not far from the thruway and I truly think the noise bothers him. He will go out on a tie-out chain in my yard, and he is totally fine with that, but a walking leash is not his thing. When he is being let out on the tie-out chain, he will only do his business if you are within sight. And, he will not stay outside alone.

He is just like a little kid to this day and he always wants to play chase. He doesn't care if you are chasing him or he is chasing you. He just loves to run. He is a Shepherd, Beagle and Terrier mix. He looks like a Shepherd, barks like a Beagle and has the energy of a Terrier. He has such a personality that everyone loves him, and I have had many people wanting my dog.

He is also smart. I have taught him many tricks over the years, including bringing me my slippers when asked to. He is a great watchdog. I do not know what I would do without my loving companion. He keeps me active. When I give him a bath, he always wants his collar back on right after. I swear he thinks it is like his jewelry or something.

I cannot stress enough how lucky we are to have him. Pet Connection is a great place!

— Kelley Fedyk

# PASQUALE

In November 2006, my husband and I decided to adopt a cat. He had been allergic in the past and was leery about getting one. I had always had several growing up and wanted one again.

I drove to Pet Connection right after work on a cold and rainy night before my husband changed his mind. When I walked in, the woman who greeted me told me to look around and let her know when I decided. After a while, I chose a black kitten. I sat down at a table to fill out the paperwork while all the free-roaming cats were playing near me. One black-and-white cat in particular caught my eye. He would jump up on the table, lay on the paperwork and knock the pen out of my hand. No matter how hard I tried to fill out the paperwork to adopt the black kitten, this cat would not let me finish.

Finally, the woman and I looked at each other and smiled, and we both knew this was the one. After I told her I was going to adopt him, he settled into my lap. She told me that she was just getting ready to take pictures of him to try to get him adopted before I came in. Apparently, he was somewhat aloof and didn't come out much. At that point I knew I made the right decision.

I brought him home and my husband and the cat have been inseparable ever since. He is the most unique cat I have ever had and everyone who meets him feels the same. He just celebrated his eleventh birthday and has some health issues, but he is still such a happy, loving cat. I am so grateful that Pasquale chose me as we honestly cannot imagine our lives without him.

— Orlando & Christine Monaco

# PEANUT

In 2008, I went to Pet Connection to look around for an addition to my family. There had been a litter of five kittens … four girls and one boy. All the girls were adopted and this handsome little orange kitten still needed a forever home. The shelter had named him Navaho, but I adopted him and renamed him Peanut.

I have had a wonderful nine years with this amazing cat and he has two brothers, Spike and Wynk, that he loves to cuddle and play with. They are all spoiled, handsome boys and I adore them!

— Valerie

# POUNCE

Hello, my name is Linda and "Tuxedo Teddy's" new name is Pounce. My granddaughter named him and I love it!

Almost a year ago I lost both of my babies within five weeks of each other. Tigger was born in my house and eighteen years later he waited for me to come home to die with me at his side. My Taz had throat cancer at 4-1/2 years old. I didn't want to get a kitten because the loss was very hard.

I've seen kittens and cats, but none called out at me until I went on Facebook and there he was — Pounce. I just knew he was the one.

I was told adopting a kitten from a rescue group was near impossible. I filled out the adoption form and waited to hear from Pet Connection. I forgot some information on the form, so I re-sent it, plus I told my whole story via email. It was a very long email!

There it was! An answer back! Could I come out and pick him up? I couldn't believe I was picked to be his new mommy! I fell in love immediately. I didn't have anything left for a kitten. I had gotten rid of everything so we had to go and buy him all kinds of things, from treats to toys, food, litter, scooper and litter box … and not forgetting a cat tree!

He is very vocal and we communicate by meowing to each other (LOL). He wants kisses, petting and love for an hour before he goes to sleep.

I could not be happier. Thank you again for picking me to love Pounce fur-ever.

— Linda Aldridge

# RILEY

Our adoption story begins with wanting a sibling for our Pug rescue, Zoe, who had separation anxiety. We went to Pet Connection in March 2009 after meeting some puppies at the Walden Galleria, but when the puppies my fiancé and I met had already been adopted, we were introduced to a litter of fifteen-week-old Lab/Hound mixes.

An adorable redhead who was coming back from a walk immediately caught our eye. We took her for a walk to the lake and we fell in love. We named her Riley after the female detective on the TV show "CSI." She was a nervous nelly who threw up on my lap on the drive home, walked behind us on walks and hid at every noise.

When we adopted her we were told she had mange but didn't realize how bad things had been for her litter and her mother, Jenny. The litter got mange and the corresponding skin infection pyoderma. Our Riley had been nicknamed by the staff as "eyeliner puppy" due to the hair loss around her eyes making it look like she had permanent eyeliner. Pet Connection was amazing in getting us the care we needed to nurse her back to health.

After months of driving back and forth to Pet Connection and the vet, the infection was gone but we were told it could come back as puppies have an impaired immune system until age two. We were holding our breath and a few months shy of her second birthday, the mange and pyoderma came back. While it was bad seeing her sick when we adopted her, it was devastating to see her fade from a healthy puppy to a sick puppy who would lay under my desk while I worked at home.

I reached out to Pet Connection and they again paid for all of her treatment! She got healthy and the infection never returned. Riley is the most lovable and gorgeous dog. Everyone who meets her comments on her sweet nature and her soft fur (at which I joke, "I guess that's what happens when all your hair falls out and has to grow back"). Although still a skittish dog, Riley's confidence built as she grew and she's happy to lead us on walks and off leash she runs with abandon.

Riley grew up with our extended family's Pugs and to this day believes she's a Pug. All fifty pounds of her wants up on your lap and will climb up with or without an invitation. Riley and her sister Zoe love each other and we love them. We've enjoyed so many memories, whether it's keeping me company on their bed in my home office, exploring new hiking spots, being "flower girls" at our wedding, participating in doggie fundraisers, pictures with Santa or just cuddling on the couch.

We are a family of four and I wouldn't have it any other way. Riley has brought so much joy to our lives and we have Pet Connection to thank for that.

— Heather Larson

# ROSCOE & MARGO

Three years ago I decided to adopt a puppy from Pet Connection. At the time I had an eight-year-old Teacup Maltese who was ill and did not have much time left. I wanted to adopt another puppy to make her life a little bit more enjoyable by having a friend. And, I was in need of another puppy because I knew the end result would be to put my Maltese down.

My stepmom referred me to Pet Connection and at the time there were about twenty puppies up for adoption, but one caught my eye and his name was Banjo. He was such an adorable puppy in the pictures I saw on Facebook! He had a white heart-shaped spot on his head and ultimately that made me decide to pick him. I filled out the application and it was accepted. I picked him up that night and he has been a part of my family ever since.

I changed his name to Roscoe and when I had to put my Maltese to sleep, having him made it so much easier to handle. He is the apple of my eye, follows me everywhere, sleeps with me, rides in the car with me and is very overprotective of me. I am so in love with him and so happy that I decided to adopt.

That little puppy once named Banjo has now grown into a three-year-old handsome doggie named Roscoe. I will forever cherish and forever be grateful that I adopted him. We have an undeniable connection that I wouldn't change for anything. I would recommend anyone that is able to adopt to do so. It made my life so much more complete.

And now I have adopted another dog from Pet Connection and her name is Margo! She is a three-year-old Pointer Hound, which is the exact same age and breed as my Roscoe. She is a loving girl who I am so happy to now have in my home. Margo and Roscoe are a match made in heaven. They are constantly flirting and are already in love with each other. I was happy to give her a home.

Margo is such a sweet girl, and it has been such an amazing experience to have adopted such an angel. She is very loving and makes life so much more enjoyable. She is one of those animals that makes you happy when you are with her and still makes you smile when you are not.

She does very funny things to Roscoe, like playfully grab his toys or smack him. I couldn't ask for more in a dog and I don't understand how anybody could give her up. When I heard her story it broke my heart and through it all she has been a happy, healthy, wonderful dog who got a second chance with a family who loves her in her forever home.

— Maura Shanley

# ROWDY

On July 9, 1994, my husband and I were married. We had just graduated from college and were just starting not only our lives together, but
adult life in general. Knowing we were too young to start a family and
being busy with graduate school, we thought a kitten would be perfect.

That August, we went to Pet Connection and saw so many beautiful kittens. However, one locked eyes with us right away and greeted us
personally. It was love at first sight and he went home with us that day. He
was the cutest, marble Tabby and we name him Rowdy after the horse in
one my favorite books, "Tex" by S.E. Hinton. It seemed to fit him because
like most kittens, he was a bundle of energy and just into everything.
From the beginning he made us laugh but he loved to snuggle, too. He
was always wherever we were in the house.

Life progressed as we finished our degrees and got new jobs. Rowdy
moved with us through three apartments and two houses. We even had
to stay with my parents for a brief time between houses. He didn't care as
long as we were together and he was always a good boy.

As the years past, our family grew. He became best friends with our seventy-five-pound flat coat Retriever and taught our two children the love of a pet. It was like we grew up together and his love was always a guide.

He was so sweet, funny and adorable with the most amazing expressions like he was listening and always understood. He was with us for good times and bad. If you were sad, his face would always cheer you up and he was quick to give comfort.

Rowdy crossed the Rainbow Bridge in 2007 but we always remember how he chose us and how lucky we were to have him in our life. He will always be our first baby and he is forever in our hearts.

— Marla Varrone

# ROXY

Roxy started out as "Lexi," a one-year-old pregnant Boxer in Virginia that was surrendered to a high-kill shelter. Her previous owners told the shelter "she ran off and got herself pregnant," so they wanted to get rid of her and get a new puppy.

One way or another, Roxy and her puppies were meant to survive, and Pet Connection came to the rescue! Roxy arrived in New York via a road trip because there was too much of a risk to fly due to icy weather conditions. She arrived just in the nick of time so that the amazing, caring people at Pet Connection could help her deliver her nine puppies.

We heard of Roxy through a volunteer after deciding we would love to bring a dog into our lives. Once her puppies were big enough to be weened from her, we were able to go meet Roxy. She was so sweet. She looked at us with sad but loving eyes and curled right up next to us on the floor. We knew immediately that she had stolen our hearts.

Today, Roxy is happy, full of energy and has so much love to give. We are so thankful for Pet Connection. Without them, we wouldn't have one of the best dogs we have ever owned.

— Dana and Shawn Weatherbee

# RUBY

I always followed Pet Connection on Facebook. Well, my daughter saw Ruby on there, my little one-eyed Pomeranian, and we had to have her. We adopted Ruby with the understanding that she was going to lose her vision in her remaining eye. Ruby has lived with us for three years now and she is very much in charge of her pack.

She has three fur siblings that outweigh her by ten and twenty pounds, and she doesn't tolerate any shenanigans. She depends on her hearing so if they play and get too loud, she tunes them right up.

Ruby still loves to go for walks and hikes. She runs into the back of my legs a lot but is just happy to be able to come along. If we run into rough terrain, she rides along in a backpack.

She maneuvers around so well that some people don't believe she is blind. Fortunately, she can hear the big dogs and just follows along.

Ruby is bossy, sassy, loving, snuggly and just a joy to have. She is so loved!

— Janice George

# RUBY

Adopting through Pet Connection was wonderful. Having eight out of ten puppies climb on you is like a dream come true. How the heck do you decide? Thank God Cheektowaga has a limit on dogs, because I would have taken all of them except the little dude chewing the wood fence in the corner. We soon picked this little girl that climbed in my soon-to-be husband's lap. We signed on all the lines and boom — she was ours.

We got all of her paperwork in a fancy Ziploc bag, food to start us off and we were wished good luck. Now came the hard part, a name. Hmmm, how about Ruby … originating from where we were engaged ten months earlier. Yup, Ruby Tuesday's in Florida while on vacation.

At first we said she was broken. She was quiet and well mannered. She got along with our other two dogs, Brandy and Daizy, but not our cat Wall-E so much. He swatted her the first day, but now they are buddies.

Well, soon enough her true Hound shined through. Stuffed animals don't stand a chance with this girl. Neither do flip flops or Wall-E's treats.

All are gone in two seconds flat or exploded into a million pieces.

At five months old it came time for Ruby's spay appointment. I saw another lady with the same iconic Ziploc bag. I thought to myself, "No way, she has Ruby's sister!" Lo and behold that lady was just as crazy as us to get one of Ella Jean's now not-so-broken pups, and come to find out, we live only minutes apart and we have the same name. Bonus!

Ruby and Koda have lots playtime together. We got the Hound part and Jess got the Vizsla. They are like day and night but when they play, it's almost like they know they are sisters.

They enjoy sharing sticks and barking at each other over the same bone. We have gone to dog parks and even met Ella Jean and several other siblings.

Jess and I attribute our friendship to our little ladies and Pet Connection for choosing us to adopt. I simply just wouldn't have it any other way.

— Joey and Jess Dabrowski and best friend Jess Taneff

# RUBY

We adopted Ruby in 2010 when she was about fifteen months old. I saw her picture online and knew right away that she was the dog for me. My husband was a bit resistant initially but eventually said we could go see her at a pet shop adoption event, but first he wanted to stop at an estate sale.

As we parked at the sale I saw Ruby in a car and thought I had missed my chance. I was so upset. We went to the event anyway and she was there! I immediately filled out the application and she came home with me that very day.

Ruby came from a shelter in Louisville, Kentucky, and we think she probably had limited experience as an indoor dog or being a real part of a family. She was a fast learner and quickly learned all of our household routines. She has been my best buddy and has really thrived these last several years. I don't think I've ever loved a dog more.

In the picture Ruby is the fawn-colored Boxer mix laying happily on the bed with her best pal Janey, another Louisville rescue. I tell people that they bark with the same regional accent!

— Megan Simpson

# RUDY

The time was right for a new friend for our black Labrador Molly, who was also a rescue. After months of searching various rescue sites, we saw a litter of pups at Pet Connection that we knew we had to go visit. Our two boys, Brian (14) and Greg (11), were really excited.

Our Molly was all black and the pups we were going to visit were grey and white. When we arrived at Pet Connection, Brian and I headed straight back to where we were told the litter we had seen on the website was. In our haste to get back to the puppies, we didn't notice that my husband and Greg didn't follow us.

Brian and I played with the pups for a while. When my husband and Greg didn't immediately follow, we went back to the front of the building to look for them. When we reached them, Greg had the most adorable black-and-white puppy in his arms. It was a tiny bit of a pup. My husband looked at Brian and I and said, "Meet Rudy … he is our new family member!"

Greg had spotted him sitting in a crate quietly and asked to hold him.

Greg is our laid back son, never asking for anything and always putting his brother's wishes before him. So when he asked my husband if we could have him, my husband couldn't say no.

It was late November, a terrible time to buy and train a puppy, but we couldn't resist. Rudy became a treasured member of our family. Rudy was named for Rudolph the Red Nosed Reindeer because it was closing in on Christmas.

We lost Rudy after he had to have major surgery and didn't make it through. I always tell people that we didn't rescue Rudy, Rudy rescued us. How we loved that boy!

Thank you for letting us honor Rudy this way.


— Kristine Blackburn

# SADIE

This is the story of my fur baby, Sadie. I was looking to adopt my very first dog of my own and had on my mind to look for a Pug. I went to the SPCA and saw two Pugs that had to be adopted together as they were brother and sister. I didn't think I could handle two dogs so I continued to look.

I found out about Pet Connection and made an appointment to view the dogs they had available. When I arrived there was a Basset Hound that had given birth to her pups recently, about two months previous. I was allowed to visit with the pups and fell in love with them. Surprisingly, not one pup looked at all like their mom as they all had Lab traits. I fell in love with them all.

That was the day my life became fulfilled with my newly adopted black Lab puppy, Sadie. She was the smartest little puppy I've ever known and after five years she is still able to learn new tricks. As a puppy, I was able to take her to work to get used to crate training, then after a few months she was able to stay at home in the crate.

Sadie has changed my life for the better; no more stress and nothing but love for her and from her on a daily basis.

Thank you, Pet Connection, for bringing so much joy to everyone who adopts from you and for taking such wonderful care of all the poor fur babies that come to you. I tell everyone about your group if they are looking to adopt a pet.

— Arlene Schall

# SADIE

My Sadie was adopted from Pet Connection in late June 2006 by my mom. We had an old dog that my Dad had found wandering the city streets in 1992 that we had to put to sleep in early June 2006.

Mom and I took a ride to Pet Connection, which is near my house. We walked around with no intention to adopt. It was only a couple of weeks since we had to put down our longtime family dog, the dog we got when I was still living at home.

We were there just to look when we spotted this friendly but timid young Shepard mix. My mom decided quickly that she wanted this dog. At the time, I had an English Bulldog who lived to be just over thirteen years old.

Around this time, my mom had to have her first knee replacement surgery and was required to spend weeks in rehab. Needless to say, mom needed help caring for Sadie. My brother took her for some time, and by the time she was having her other knee replaced, I had put my old English Bulldog to rest. I began taking Sadie on occasional walks and spending a great deal of time with her. I would then take her Thursday through Sunday.

For the past six years, I've dropped her off every morning and then pick her up after work. Sadie has two homes with two of everything. She is now approximately thirteen years old and I walk her at Elma Park, Marilla Town Park and through the Marilla Cemetery just about daily. When people see her they think she is a young dog. She looks great but she just started to have hearing issues. She has always been a friendly dog that everyone just adores. She is my best friend and I hope I can keep her healthy for many more years. She is the perfect dog!

Sadie also loves cats, but unfortunately lost her best friend Sammy, an orange Tabby, this past March.

— Colleen Czechowski

# SADIE

In July of 2010 we adopted Sadie from Pet Connection. She was a maternity rescue who had recently given birth.

Sadie is a Beagle mix with the sweetest disposition. She loves her daily walks, playing and cuddling with us.

It is so wonderful to adopt rescue pets for they are forever grateful.

— Kate & Jerry Seweryniak

# SADIE

My son was asking for a dog every day for at least two years. He even made a chart of all his friends who had dogs and two videos of why our family should have a dog with charts and graphs. He even dressed in a suit for the presentation.

So without his knowledge I started searching online. I could have gone to the Buffalo dog pound but we had a Beagle from there with separation issues and my son is autistic so I wanted to start with a puppy and see how much we could make her into a support-type dog for my son.

I searched the Petfinder website and found a picture of "Sunny's Gang." The pictures were of a mom and about five puppies. I fell in love and immediately emailed Pet Connection for an application. I waited to hear back for three days. Nothing.

I then found them on Facebook and pictured on the page was the "Gang" and a super sweet video of the puppies, so I contacted them again. There were so many comments and likes on the pictures that I figured I had no chance. I contacted Pet Connection again and I received an email with the application and I poured my heart into it. After I submitted the application, I got a pretty quick response. No. I was crushed!

I learned a valuable lesson that day. Puppies need constant attention and couldn't be left in a crate while I went to work part-time without being let out or played with. I did some fancy footwork and got my neighbor and mom-in-law to agree to come over for puppy play time until I was off for the summer and could take over. I emailed Pet Connection back. Sorry, no dice.

So I went back to Petfinder and I really didn't have the heart to get attached to another puppy. It was a half-hearted search. The following day was Sunday and I was depressed but couldn't tell the family why. Then, a miracle happened! I received an email from Pet Connection at 6:30 at night that asked if I still wanted the puppy. What? Of course I definitely still wanted the puppy!

The email said they had only one puppy left. She was female and her name was Rain. Could I come to Pet Connection the next day, Monday? I would have driven over right at that moment but I agreed to Monday afternoon. My husband met me at Pet Connection and we went in together.

The super nice lady who was there stated she was not the regular adoption lady. We were totally wrong in assuming we were there to be interviewed. We chatted for a bit, I held Rain in my arms and the nice lady said, "So, do you want her?" In my mind I thought, "Are you kidding? Of course!" We both calmly signed the papers and never let Rain go.

I drove home while Rain slept in the seat next to me and when we got home, my husband walked in the house first and started talking to the kids about their day. Then I came in with Rain. The squeals, happy tears and jumps for joy were more than enough for me to know that she was the perfect fit.

Rain is now Sadie, a Labrador, Boxer, Collie mix who is high energy, healthy, happy and definitely a welcome member of our family. We made big plans for her first birthday in September 2017 with a party and doggie treats. Thank you for helping me pull off one of the best surprises ever!

— Tammy, Mark, Matthew and Elizabeth Nunciato

# SOPHIA

I adopted Sophia on December 18, 2012. She was born on October 17, 2012. I remember seeing her laying there, looking so calm with this little wrinkle in her forehead. There were so many puppies it was hard to choose. As anyone can imagine I wanted to take them all home with me. But as soon as I saw her, I held her and that wrinkle got me.

The day I brought her home was one of the best days of my life. It did not take her long to warm up and make herself at home. She was so tiny — about the length of my forearm — and when she looked at me my heart melted. It was so fun to watch her personality come alive in just a day. Sadly, she grew into that wrinkle on her forehead. However, it does come out every now and again.

I already had an elderly dog, Sage, and she was slowing down, but as soon as I brought Sophia home it was like she gave new life to Sage. At that moment I knew Sophia was meant to be with us. Sophia loves being outside (in the wintertime, too), going for walks and playing sometimes with toys, but the majority of the time she just likes to wrestle. She is such a good girl; she will just sit in the yard and hang out and watch what I am doing.

I knew she was a Terrier mix but as she grew, you can tell she was part Chihuahua. Her nickname is Chalupa because if you saw her you would say the same thing. Some of her expressions are priceless. For example, if we are laying down and I move her she gets a mad look. Or, if I am eating something she knows is good, she gets that wrinkle back in her forehead and it kills me.

Sophia makes such a great addition to my home, and she truly is my best friend. I am forever thankful for all the hard work Pet Connection does to save the lives of cats and dogs. If it wasn't for them I'd be missing out on all the joy and happiness Sophia brings to my life.

— Jill Lach

# TEDDY

We adopted Teddy from Pet Connection in Marilla in October of 2009. Those puppies had a great little story of their own. Pet Connection was assisting New Orleans with their displaced animals left from Hurricane Katrina and its aftermath.

It was the first time the shelter had both mom and dad on the premises. By the time they made it to New York, "Tyco" the Border Collie and "Garcia" the Shepherd-Collie mix were about to be parents. Tyco was adopted out but Garica was an extremely large, sweet dog who ended up staying at the shelter as their mascot. I kept in touch with the shelter, exchanging stories about how Teddy and his father had similar traits of rolling on the floor talking (howling).

I loved Teddy like he was my baby. He attended obedience classes where he excelled in every command they taught him and graduated with top honors in his class. He was such a happy dog with a lot of personality. There was not a person that met him that didn't love him. He was a constant reminder for me to be the person he thought I was.

Teddy brought such joy to our family. Unfortunately, we lost Teddy to lymphoma on June 28th of this year. There will never be another dog quite like my sweet boy. My kids are anxious to fill the void left behind with another dog but I think it's going to take some more time.

— Janice Joyce

# TEDDY

I found my Bella (a Border Collie/Lab mix) at Pet Connection in 2012 and felt she should have another canine to hang around with because it only seemed right to me that she shouldn't be the only dog in a house with two cats. She needed a buddy of her own that was like her — someone who spoke her language.

I started looking on the Pet Connection website and saw quite a few dogs and puppies that needed a good home, but I was a little leery because the house was pretty harmonious as it was and I didn't want to ruin things.

Then I saw a litter of Pomeranians in 2013 that a little girl named Ruby had given birth to and I'm sure I never have seen anything cuter in my whole life. I silently watched the little puppy pictures that would get posted occasionally on the Pet Connection website and wrestled with the idea of introducing a little one like that to my Bella.

I was on vacation when the Poms went up for adoption and was happy that there was a little guy left when I got back. He was all by himself after having two brothers and three sisters as part of his original pack. I felt sad for him and didn't want him to be lonely so I brought Bella back to where I adopted her for a meeting to see if she approved of this little rascal. The meet-and-greet went pretty well so we took him home the same day I got back from vacation.

His name was Jiffy but I renamed him Teddy. Teddy was pretty shy at first but that didn't last long.

Teddy is gorgeous — and I think he knows it — and weighs just sixteen pounds but he doesn't know how small he is for he is not afraid of anything. I keep a close eye on him to keep him out of trouble.

Teddy likes to lay on his back on the cool floor in the hallway with his legs straight up in the air when he's resting during the day, but at night he lays in the hallway where he can see all three bedroom doors as well as the front door and guards us all.

He understands commands but is stubborn and gives me a hard time. In 2015 he went to obedience class and got a ribbon for most improved.

He learned how to catch a small Frisbee and he can catch a rubber ball with holes. He loves to be brushed and combed and he runs really fast.

I was very surprised to see how quick he is and it is hilarious to watch him run faster than his forty-pound herding sister. My husband and I laughed hard when Teddy chased Bella and playfully bit her tail. Bella was shocked, too.

This guy is a protective watchdog and a loving part of the family. I'm very happy to have Teddy in my life thanks to Pet Connection!

— Terri Smith

# TEDDY

After grieving for a couple of months after putting our first precious, furry, four-legged family member to rest, my father, brother, sister and I were waiting for my mother's approval as to when she was ready to get another dog.

One day in August while at work, my phone was continuously going off, receiving calls and texts from my brother. I began to get worried so I went to another room where I saw a picture of a puppy that said, "Do you mind if we get him?" I immediately called my brother back without hesitation while in shock. Thankfully, my shift was just about finished so I clocked out and instantly began to cry as I ran to my car. To this day, I am still unsure as to how I made it home safely since tears were streaming down my face.

When I arrived home, I called my family who said they were on their way home with our new family puppy and to get materials ready for him. I quickly gathered a blanket, pillows and water and made my way outside to our driveway, pacing up and down as I waited for them to arrive. The tears just continued to stream down my face and I could barely contain my excitement!

About ten minutes later the tears finally stopped. But as I saw our family car begin to turn the corner and pull into our driveway, the tears immediately started streaming down again! Before the car came to a complete stop, my sister, who was holding the puppy, rolled down the window for me to see him and I could not believe how precious he was. I swung the door open, took him from my sister's arms and began noticing every perfect little detail about him.

Later that night, my family spent hours trying to decide on a name for our new pup, and after much discussion, Theodore was chosen and we would call him Teddy.

Ever since that day, our family was complete again and that much closer since Teddy has created a bond between us that is so special. Teddy has continuously provided each of us with love as he cuddles, kisses and nuzzles us many times each day. Our family now has more inside jokes and stories that we share daily with each other that revolve around Teddy. He gives us so much unconditional love, happiness, joy and companionship throughout each day.

Teddy has the biggest "boy" personality that keeps us all on our toes, "cha-cha" dances after taking care of his business during walks, and is always there to greet us at the door. Our lives changed for the better the moment Teddy was picked up from Pet Connection, and we are and will continue to be forever grateful and blessed to have him as a member of our family.

— Rebecca Mercuri

# TEENA

Our adoption from Pet Connection was one of the best decisions we ever made.

As an animal lover, especially animals in need, I am constantly looking at websites for dogs that need help or a new home. One particular day I was on Facebook and my friend that used to live in Marilla but now lives in Florida had a picture of "Dreama" with a post stating, "Someone please go get her!"

That was it for us. I showed my husband the picture of her and he said, "Let's go!" Now I was a bit shocked at his remark and reaction as he usually just says "cute" because he knows if he said yes to every dog I showed him we would have way too many. He even took the initiative to call the shelter to see if we could go and meet her.

Luckily, they were available for us to come right out. I was so excited it was hard to sit still for the hour ride.

When Dreama first came out she was so happy, almost looking like she was smiling. Her tail never stopped wagging. It didn't take us long to decide that she was going to be the newest addition to our family.

I still remember when we told the helper that we wanted to take her home with us, she said, "Oh, she has been waiting so long." My heart nearly broke. She called Dreama from the other room and she came running out right to us and got into our car. I took a picture of her on my lap and sent it to my friend in Florida. She was so excited that we adopted her and said it was the best message she ever got!

On our way home we decided that her name would be "Teena Marie" and she immediately started responding to it. While Teena is not a kisser, she gives the most awesome hugs I have ever had. Teena has two acres on which to run and a spot on our bed where she lays on her back to have her belly rubbed every night.

She has been a loving and very important part of our lives for the past five years and we would do it all over again in a heartbeat!

— Marcia & Michael Flower

# THUNDER

Thunder was adopted in 1994 from Pet Connection. When we first met Thunder, he was in a pen with his brothers and sisters. I was tasked with picking out the next member of our family.

I was drawn to Thunder's brown spots above his eyes and I knew immediately that he would be perfect and so loved, so we brought him home. Of course we were prepared for the normal puppy misbehavior, but Thunder was truly one of a kind. He was a Rottweiler/German Shepherd mix and a strong and large puppy. A few of Thunder's antics included getting through the metal bars of his cage while we were out of the house, destroying furniture and rugs, eating chalk and other items that should not be consumed (he was sneaky), etc. It was so bad that we thought about bringing him back to Pet Connection.

But as we were all in the car ready to return him, my sisters and I were crying our eyes out. We knew that Thunder could never be taken back. He had a permanent place in our home and our hearts. As Thunder grew older, he became more calm and docile, extremely lovable and was like another person — not just a furry friend. He weighed over one hundred pounds!

Thunder understood every word we would say to him. He knew instinctively when we were sad and he would lick our tears away as they fell. As the years went by, eight-year-old Thunder had to have knee surgery. I remember going to school and wondering if he would make it out of surgery because he was older. When I got off the bus and walked in the door, I'll never forget seeing him with the cone around his neck and running up to him as he laid there wagging his tail. I was forever thankful that my boy was still there and that I could continue to love him.

Thunder recovered, but we knew he would not live forever. We cared for him, built him a ramp to take pressure off his leg and gave him all the love and attention we possibly could. Thunder wanted for nothing. But one day, as we let Thunder outside, we found out he could not get up. He laid on the grass and we knew that Thunder had taken his final walk. We stayed with him throughout the night on our patio — sitting with him, loving him, crying with him. We knew that as the morning came, we would need to say goodbye to our brother, son, forever friend.

As we cherished those final moments and as sad and heartbreaking as it was to say goodbye to him, we took solace knowing that he knew he was loved, that he knew we had given him a wonderful life, and that he knew he touched each one of our hearts because the bond and love that we all had with Thunder was one in a million. He was a fantastic dog that we will carry in our hearts forever.

— Ashley Ann Czechowski

# TIGER & BAILEY

When we bought our house in June 2009, I knew that we would eventually get a dog. So, until we were ready, I decided to volunteer with Pet Connection. A year later, I saw a picture online of a litter of puppies that were coming up for adoption. I showed the picture to my daughter and she fell in love with one of the furry faces. We decided we were ready for a new family member and decided to apply.

The furry face that captured my daughter's heart belonged to our beautiful Tiger girl, a Shepherd-Husky mix. Without a doubt, Tiger was the smartest dog that had ever lived with me. She loved playing in her baby pool in the summer, Frosty Paws and us.

When Tiger was one year old, she was diagnosed with a mast cell tumor. She had surgery at Cornell University Hospital for Animals. While they successfully removed the whole tumor, mast cell tumors are infamous for returning. While we didn't see any signs of the recurrence of the tumor, in October 2015 we lost our beloved Tiger to cancer.

In May 2016, while bottle-feeding Babe's puppies at Pet Connection, there was another litter of pups — Anna's pups — that I helped to socialize. I fell in love with all the doggies and talked to my family about adding a puppy to our household. In July, when the puppies were ready to find homes, my daughter, her fiancé, my granddaughter and I went to Pet Connection to pick out our puppy. My future son-in-law, who had never picked out a dog of his own, chose Bailey for our family.

Bailey was one of Anna's pups and is a Collie (maybe Shepherd, maybe Hound ... who knows) mix. Bailey is a big, goofy boy and we love him dearly. He loves his little girl (and all of us), being outside, playing tug, running and playing with his dog cousin Rita, eating treats and, if he gets in the house with wet paws, sliding all over the floors. Bailey has added much joy and laughter to our home. It is so true that a house is not a home without a dog!

— Joanne Cruce

# TRIXIE

Greyhounds were the breed of choice for our family for more than a decade. Then we lost one and then another to cancer ... and then our two children came along before our third Greyhound passed.

Suddenly, our home didn't feel complete without a fur baby. That's when I started my search for a new companion.

I spent hours scoping out websites, adoption groups and stalking available dogs online. Then I saw a picture of a momma dog, Sandy, who was available for adoption on Pet Connection's website. I read about her and fell in love with her cute face. A Jack Russel Terrier mix was a far cry from a Greyhound, but I couldn't resist!

Next came the part where I had to approach the subject with my husband. The kids were all on board and luckily so was my husband, so off we went to meet her.

Sandy was busy being a watchful mother over her puppies when we first met her but she would have been happy to leave with us if she could have that first day. After having met her, we completed the papers to adopt her and waited for her to be able to leave her puppies. When we picked her up, she left happily, jumped in our van and fell asleep on her new blanket for the ride home.

Now to my favorite story to tell. Once we got home, I walked her around the house on a leash to introduce her to her new home. I had a big fluffy pillow set up for her in front of the fireplace in the family room. I walked her over to it, sat down next to it and patted the pillow telling her how it was just for her. She sniffed it, then walked right over it to my lap where she promptly sat down. I laughed and thought, "So this is how it's going to be?"

Well, almost four years later Trixie (we changed her name) is my constant shadow. She follows me from room to room, beats me to the couch and curls up on me or next to me wherever I am. Such unconditional love and companionship!

She is the most perfect addition to our family and has come a long way since we brought her home. We can't imagine our lives without our girl!

— Michelle Moore

# TUCKER

This story began in 2009. My parents and I had gone to the mall and happened to see Pet Connection there with four little puppies. I was sixteen and wanted nothing more than a new puppy in our house. I begged and pleaded, but my mom said no. My dad said he'd work on it with her.

I was relentless the next month. I kept asking her and sending pictures and I kept my eye on these puppies. The day came where they went up for adoption and we had decided to go for it.

My mom went to the shelter and wrote as fast as she could to get one of the gorgeous puppies. She succeeded and I got to name him. His name is Tucker James.

This dog has the greatest personality of a puppy that I have ever known. He loves to go in the pool, he loves sleeping with his dad, and he loves treats. He would sleep with me daily.

Rescuing him was what began my love for rescue shelters. Tucker is brilliant. He is an alpha male and runs the house. Up until five months ago he was the youngest of four dogs but you'd never know it. He was in charge, but he loved his siblings to no end. Up until I left for college he was my dog and slept with me every night.

An unforeseen bond happened once I left. My dad and Tucker developed an inseparable bond, and to this day they are still inseparable. They sleep together, watch TV together, eat together, go on walks together, go on car rides together and make each other's lives better. They are best friends.

Tucker may have been born in a shelter, but he now is the king of his castle and we wouldn't have it any other way.

— Jordan Dudish

# TYLER

We started our journey with Pet Connection ten years ago. My daughter had been wanting a kitten after the loss of her cat she had since she was four. We looked at other places and couldn't find the perfect match so I went online and discovered Pet Connection.

That day I picked the kids up from school and we were on our way. We entered the facility and were directed to a room of kittens up for adoption. We knew we wanted a female kitten so after finding the most adorable little girl kitty we were sure we had found the one. However, after spending more time with her she wasn't quite as affectionate and friendly as we had hoped.

Everyone was quite disappointed after traveling about an hour and coming that close. We decided to keep looking and were about to leave when we noticed an adorable black-and-white kitten curled up in bed. The woman told us he was the brother to the girl kitten we had been looking at. They had been found in a cardboard box at a gas station were someone had left them.

The male had singed whiskers and the girl had a broken tail. I can't understand how people can be so cruel. We had to snuggle that poor kitten before we headed back home. As he looked up we found he had a perfect heart-shaped nose. Why couldn't this be a girl kitty?

That's when the magic happened! He was calm and super lovable and continually purred. We thought maybe we would give his sister another chance but she ran from us. My husband was persistent about having a female kitten because he had heard how male cats will spray everything in your house.

I could see the bond that was happening as my daughter held him and how sweet he was. I began asking more detailed questions about male cat tendencies. I was told that spraying wasn't a common problem unless there was another cat in the household, which there wasn't.

The longer we stayed the more the love grew between this adorable male kitten and my family. After a lot of discussion we decided there was no way we would be leaving without this kitten, that was given the name Tyler. We went through the adoption process and it has been a perfect fit ever since. He is loving and social and has melted many non cat lovers' hearts.

We have always had at least two dogs living here and many other daily dog visitors. Tyler grooms the dogs and is always looking for a vacant lap to snuggle on. He greets visitors as they enter our home. He has never sprayed or damaged anything. He actually goes for walks on a harness and leash with the rest of his canine and human family. He is a large part of our family and we love him very much!

Thank you, Pet Connection!

— Lynn Sickler

# WINNIE

We adopted Winnie, a cute little Hound mix puppy, from Pet Connection in June 2014. She is extremely friendly and is constantly complimented for her sweet temperament. She loves to meet new people and make dog friends on her long walks, but she also loves time at home playing with toys and sleeping under the covers.

We just celebrated her third birthday and are so happy that we brought this little girl home!

— Jaime Mathiebe

# WINSTON

In April of 2014, my parents and I were given the opportunity to adopt a puppy from the Pet Connection shelter. After hearing about their shelter on Facebook and seeing the efforts that were made to save pregnant strays and find good homes for the mothers and their babies, I felt immediately compelled to talk to my parents about submitting an application for the adoption of some very adorable Lab/Beagle mix puppies from Merit's litter.

However, this decision did not come without resistance as my parents and I were still recovering from the heartbreaking passing of our twelve-year-old Beagle during the previous summer. She had been the only family dog we ever had, welcoming her into our family when I was only six. All three of us (but especially my dad) were hesitant to open our hearts to another dog, but I strongly felt that the time was right.

When we found out we were one of the families selected to take home a puppy, we couldn't wait for the day to come! My mom and I nervously but excitedly arrived at our appointment time (new leash and toys in hand) with four puppies left for us to choose from. I immediately was drawn to one of the two males left, and with a silly sounding grunt as my mom picked him up, he gave her a couple of sloppy kisses on the cheek and the deal was sealed.

Winston was the name we had picked out for him, and with some very helpful closing information from the volunteers at Pet Connection, we were out the door and on our way home. Winston was understandably confused at first but quickly made himself very comfortable at home with us and his new feline brother, Journey.

From the first day home, Winston began to steal our hearts with his strongly vivacious personality and proved to be the perfect addition to our family. Winston continues to steal our hearts every day. He is very noisy and loves to "talk" to us and make sure he is heard. His favorite thing is to be outside, no matter if it is the summer or winter, but he especially loves the snow. He doesn't seem to have grown out of his puppy stage and loves running around as much as he can and loves to play fetch, but hates giving the ball back. A few of his other favorite things are ripping up toys we buy him, looking out the window, making friends with guests and new people, cuddling, and "helping" dad do chores outside and in the house.

We can't imagine our lives now without the joy that Winston brings to us every day, and we are so grateful for the opportunity that Pet Connection has given us to give Winston the best possible life and care that he can have, and to also have our lives enriched by the love and happiness that having Winston provides for us on a daily basis!

— Colleen Lukasik

# WINTER

I first met Winter back in May of 2015. I work at the Bennington Vet Clinic where Pet Connection always brings their pets. When Winter came in she had heartworm disease, Ehrlichia canis (a tick-borne disease) and an ear infection.

Winter's puppies were seven weeks old at the time and they had to be weaned in order for treatment to begin. Winter came to our office frequently for treatment and she never made a fuss no matter what we had to do.

The months went on and everyone at work started to call Winter my dog. In October of 2015 we adopted Winter into our family once I convinced my husband that she was already my dog. Now Winter loves laying on the couch and rolling in the dirt every chance she gets!

— Sarah Shuknecht

# ZOEY

My boyfriend Matt and I had been talking about adopting a dog off and on for a few months. In October 2013, we began following just about every adoption and rescue organization in Western New York knowing it was important to us to adopt a dog who was in need of a loving home. Pet Connection Programs Inc. of Marilla stood out to us especially when we learned they were a maternity shelter, taking in mothers and their pups to make sure they find good homes.

Scrolling through Facebook, our news feeds soon became filled with adorable faces and big, sad eyes of dogs begging to be adopted. Knowing there were so many dogs whose hearts were filled with love to give made it so difficult for us to choose when to finally apply for one.

One evening, a Facebook post with photos of three adorable pups brought the biggest smile to my face. Described as "a very short Doxie mix," the pups had long but little six-pound bodies and short legs with the face of a Terrier. They looked like curious and playful little sweeties. I immediately filled out an application and, to my excitement, quickly heard back from Pet Connection and was told to come in over the next couple of days.

When I told Matt I had sent in an application and that we could go see these puppies in a day or so, he was excited and also a bit cautious knowing there was a possibility they may not be the right fit. When we got to the shelter we learned that two black, scruffy puppies were left, along with another litter of adorable Boxer-Pit mix puppies. We played with the puppy named Button who we had our eye on from the photos, who was also in the center of all the puppy action.

After a few minutes of searching, we finally found her sister Bean outside in the back yard enjoying her own little toy in a huge doghouse that made her look even smaller than her six pounds. She looked up at us as we approached and welcomed some playtime as she shared her toy with us. Her tail wagged and her extra-long body squirmed as we played together, her big brown eyes smiling up at us. Matt and I looked at each other and knew she chose us.

We signed the papers, bundled up our new family member in the blankets we brought and drove back home to North Buffalo. I can't even begin to describe the amount of joy Bean, now Zoey, has brought to our lives. We share so many fun memories with our baby girl. She has the funniest personality as she trots around the house with her favorite rubber duck. When friends invite us over, they know we will always ask, "Can baby Zoey come too?"

Our little "Rolly-Polly Zoey" loves perching up on Matt's shoulders while we sit on our patio chairs, knows the location of her favorite orange ball throughout the house at all times, sprawls out on her back as she basks in the sun and never fails to give us both kisses every day. She has been so central to our lives that we made sure to include her in our wedding photos by making a special stop at our home to capture some moments with her on one of the best days of our lives. We cherish every moment we have with Zoey and are so grateful Pet Connection Programs Inc. of Marilla introduced us to our fur baby.

— Samantha and Matt Pacana

# ZOLA

In January of last year, a friend of mine expressed interest in getting a therapy dog from Pet Connection. I took a look at the picture of the pups that she was trying to adopt and instantly knew I wanted one for myself. I sent an application that day and soon after had an appointment to meet the two puppies available for adoption.

When we walked into the pen, this girl immediately claimed us as her own. She didn't stop licking me the entire time and she was super gentle and loving with my two little boys. We took her home that day and are so happy to have added her to our family.

We named her Zola (her name used to be Avalanche). She now has a big fur brother named Zeus who is eight years old. They get along very well. Actually, when we separate them the howling gets out of control! I wonder what the neighbors think?

Zola is very protective of her humans. We can't play or wrestle or even pick up our kids and throw them around anymore without her protective barking telling us to knock it off. She is the sweetest dog I have ever met, very kind-hearted and eager to please. We just love her!

— Nina Szarafin

# About the Author

Joe Kirchmyer has enjoyed writing and story-telling since an early age. He earned a bachelor's degree in journalism from Buffalo State College and after graduation went to work for several weekly newspapers in the Western New York area before starting a three-year stint in corporate marketing. He later joined The Buffalo News where he worked for 20 years and oversaw the production of countless special sections and advertisements.

In 2009 he fulfilled a lifelong dream and opened his own small business, a communications company called Kirchmyer Media LLC. The company, based in Joe's hometown of West Seneca, New York, caters to the communication needs of nonprofit organizations and other small businesses throughout Western New York and Southern Ontario.

Joe's previous books, all published by NFB Publishing in Buffalo, New York, include *Diamonds in the Rough*, a compilation of short stories with sports and inspirational themes; *Most Likely to Survive*, detailing the incredible story of Matthew Faulkner, a young man who overcame long odds to recover from a significant traumatic brain injury; and *Head, Heart & Hands: Continuing the Handcrafted Tradition of the Original Roycroft Artisans*. Joe has also provided writing and photography services for a large number of other books, publications and websites.

In addition to writing, Joe enjoys photography, collecting, sports, the great outdoors and dogs, of course! He is also the co-owner of the popular website BuffaloScoop.com.

To contact Joe or to schedule an interview or speaking engagement, please send an email to *jkirchmyer@verizon.net.*

## About the Cover

The painting used for the cover of this book was graciously provided by Cheektowaga, New York artist Ken Newton, the proud owner of two Pet Connection rescue dogs! Bo is a ten-year-old Beagle/Terrier mix and Albert is a six-year-old Golden Lab. They are named after professional baseball players Bo Jackson and Albert Pujols.

For more information on Ken Newton Studios, please visit his Facebook page at *www.facebook.com/KenNewtonStudios*.

Made in the USA
Las Vegas, NV
29 July 2021